REAL MEN ~~TALKING~~ Joking!!

Other books by Allan M. Nixon

Beaut Utes
Beaut Utes Calendar 2000
Stand and Deliver: 100 Australian Bushrangers
Humping Bluey: Swagmen of Australia
Pocket Positives: An A–Z of Inspirational Quotations
The Swagmen: Survivors of the Great Depression
The Grinham Report: A Family History
100 Australian Bushrangers: 1789–1901
Inglewood Gold 1859-1982
Muddy Boots:Inglewood Football Club
Inglewood: Gold Town of Early Victoria

REAL MEN ~~TALKING~~ Joking!!

Compiled by
Allan M. Nixon

Lothian
BOOKS

DEDICATED TO GLEN STEVENS 1949–98
One of the funniest buggers I ever knew. He had the ability to make you laugh when no one else could. Missed by all his mates at Telstra, Golden Square Football Club, numerous pubs and by many people in many places,
and
SPECIAL THANKS TO BILLY CONNOLLY,
master storyteller, hilarious Scotsman and rude bugger.
May the laughing bird always make its nest near you.

Thomas C. Lothian Pty Ltd
11 Munro Street, Port Melbourne, Victoria 3207

Copyright © Allan M. Nixon 1999
First published 1999

All rights reserved. No part of this publication may be reproduced, stored in a retrieval system or transmitted in any form by any means without the prior permission of the copyright owner. Enquiries should be made to the publisher.

National Library of Australia
Cataloguing-in-Publication data:

Nixon, Allan M., 1951–.
  Real men talking
  ISBN 0 7344 0061 6.
  1. Australian wit and humor.
  A828.302

Design and cartoons by Geoff Hocking
Printed in Australia by Griffin Press Pty Limited

INTRO

Some of the following pages will be about as popular as a tampon in a bloke's thermos! This book will offend, be seen as sexist, politically incorrect, insulting, derogatory and downright bloody rude. Hopefully, it will also give you a bit of a laugh.

How did this book come about? We were in Burkie's big shed on his farm. A good winter's fire was going in a 44-gallon drum cut in half. The cement floor of the shed was littered with empty beer cans, and full ones kept appearing as they usually do in Burkie's shed. Two dogs, Mongrel's Murphy and Burkie's Tippy, renewed their friendship and wagged their approval of proceedings.

R. A. G. (Rough-as-Guts) Engineering was in business. Before us lay the steel formations of a new trailer that the two boys were welding for me. Stopping for a break, all three of us sat talking and subjects all and sundry came forth. Mongrel would say something, which Burkie would expand on with his lightning fast wit, then Mongrel would respond. And back and forth it went.

The idea for a book was revolving in my head. In almost any Aussie shed in just about any town or farm, there's a fair chance you'll find your own Mongrel and Burkie. You have heard of Abbott and Costello, Hitler and Goering. Now you'll know Mongrel and Burkie. I claim these two reprobates as my own verbal tonic — may they continue for many years (and cans) to come. Thanks fellas, the cheque is in the mail.

I walked into a bookstore for a browse and found forty-seven joke books — by 'professional' joke tellers, TV and radio celebrities, and the like. The first book I looked at had about thirty jokes I had heard before and most of them were pretty crude. I wondered how the hell was I going to compete. Well, the end result is before you; I hope it will fill a small gap in the thirst for things to make the days go by.

This collection comes from people from all walks of life, from offices, pubs, emails, faxes, and from one end of the country to the other. Invariably, when you ask someone for a joke, chances are it will be a rude one.

Crude, lewd and downright rude sums up this collection. We really are a rude pack of bastards!

I haven't been able to credit all my sources. I usually know who wrote or said it, but they don't want anyone to know. Sometimes I'm stuffed if I know who wrote it; or I made it up, but don't want to be attributed with it; or I pinched it from somewhere but can't remember where; or I'm too lazy to spend more time researching who said or wrote it first. Plagiarism is when you pinch from one source; good research is when you pinch from many sources; and this is a bloody well-researched book!

Thanks anyway to all those people who took the time to tell me their favourite jokes. Many people also took the time to email me jokes, and special mention must go to Toohey, one of the Utedogs Dart Team, from the Blue Mountains.

Further south in the suburbs at the base of the Dandenongs, near Melbourne, Wanga went beserk and flooded my email site, one joke even sending me into a spin, as it appeared to be a virus that would stuff my computer. Thankfully it didn't.

Fordgirl's mate Jockstrap did pretty well, rattling them off the top of his head like a machine gun. Mongrel and his mate Burkie started off OK, but they didn't have the stamina to continue. Thanks also to Bazza of Bendigo and Leslie D.A.D., who kept the Telstra fax running hot. Thanks also to Anakie, and his mate The O' Man.

To all yarn spinners not individually named due to space, my thanks for your efforts. May the shining light of mirthdom always rest its rays upon you all.

I've always been a lousy joke teller. I thought if I wrote all these yarns down on paper, I'd remember them and become the life of the party. It didn't work and I still have to read them, but at least these jokes are in alphabetical order.

I'd love to hear your jokes, so post them to me at PO Box 46, North Essendon, Vic. 3041 and I may include them in a possible future book.

Be warned this book may cause interference to your pacemaker, so click it up a notch or two, and you may survive this lot. Relax with a tinnie in the deckchair, or take the book to the dunny for a browse.

And may the elastic on your jockstrap never be too tight!

Ooroo!

Allan 'The Uteman' Nixon

ADAM

Adam's first mistake was listening to Eve,
and we've been paying for it ever since.

After God had created Adam he noticed that he looked very lonely. He decided to help. He said 'Adam, I've decided to make you a woman. She'll love you, cook for you, be sweet to you, and understand you.'

Adam said, 'Great! How much will she cost me?'
The answer came back, 'An arm and a leg.'
'Well,' said Adam, 'What can I get for a rib?'

AEROPLANE SEX

A mother and her son were flying Ansett from Perth to Melbourne. The son, who had been looking out the window, turned to his mother and said, 'If big dogs have baby dogs, and big cats have baby cats, why don't big planes have baby planes?'

His mother couldn't think of an answer, so told her son to ask the flight attendant. So the boy asked the flight attendant, 'If big dogs have baby dogs, and big cats have baby cats, why don't big planes have baby planes?'

The surprised flight attendant asked, 'Did your mother tell you to ask me?' When the boy nodded, she said, 'Tell your mother that Ansett always pulls out on time.'

As an aeroplane is about to crash, a female passenger jumps up frantically and announces, 'If I am going to die, I want to die feeling like a woman.' She removes all her clothes and asks, 'Is there any-

one on this plane man enough to make me feel like a woman?'

A man stands up, takes off his shirt, and says, 'Here, iron this!'

AFFAIR

Geoff had been having an affair with a woman for a few months, and one night he fell asleep and woke very late.

'Shit, Mary I've got to go, my wife will kill me, I should have been home hours ago. Get some talcum powder, quick.'

He rushed home to find his wife in the lounge fuming. 'Where have you been?' she said.

'Oh, I've had a night of passionate sex with this gorgeous blonde, and then got stuck in a traffic jam.'

'Oh yeah? In your dreams. Let me see your hands.'

Geoff obliged.

'I knew I was right,' said his wife. 'You've been out to that bloody bowling alley with your drunken mates again!'

AIDS

What do an AIDS patient and the man you caught in bed with your wife have in common?

They have both screwed themselves into an early grave.

ALL-OVER TAN

There once was a man who really took care of his body. One day, he took a look in the mirror and noticed that he was tan all over except for his penis. He decided to do something about it. He went to the beach, stripped naked and buried himself in the sand, except for his penis which he left sticking out.

Two old women were strolling along the beach, one using a cane. Seeing the penis sticking up out of the sand, she began to move it around with her cane, remarking to the other old woman, 'There's no justice in the world.'

The second old woman asked what she meant.

'Well,' she answered, 'When I was 20, I was curious about it. When I was 30, I enjoyed it. When I was 40, I asked for it. When I was 50, I paid for it. When I was 60, I begged for it. When I was 70, I prayed for it.

When I was 80 I forgot about it.

'Now, I am 90 and the damn things are growing wild on the beach, and I'm too old to squat.'

ANAL SEX

Why do some men prefer anal sex?
Because it is warmer, tighter, and more degrading to the woman.

ANATOMY

In an anatomy class, a young blonde woman is asked by her professor to name three of the most important parts of the male body.

'Um, first is the brain, second the heart,' she says. She stops and a puzzled look appears on her face. 'Third is, … um, I've had it on my fingertips, I had it on the tip of my tongue, oh, I've had it drilled into me a thousand times, … now, what was it …'

APPEARANCE

Why do women spent more time on their appearance than improving their mind?
Because men may be stupid but they aren't blind.

AROUSED?

How do you tell if a woman is sexually aroused?
Put your hand in her panties to see if it feels like a horse eating oats.

ARTHUR AND EMILY

They had been married for 50 years and are seated at the breakfast table. Emily reminisces, 'Arthur, remember when we were young and we used to sit at the breakfast table in the nude?'

Arthur nearly chokes on his toast, 'Emily! Do you mind? Not while I'm eating breakfast.'

'C'mon, dear, we're not too old. Get your pyjamas off.'

A spark comes into Arthur's eyes, as he remembers the good old days. Minutes later, there they sit, both stark naked.

'Oh Arthur. You still get me hot and bothered — after all these years.'

Arthur looks over his glasses, and says, 'I'm not surprised you're hot. You've got one tit in your tea and the other in your porridge!'

AUCTIONS

Wife: 'I dreamt they were auctioning off dicks. The big ones went for ten dollars and the thick ones went for twenty dollars.'
Husband: 'How about the ones like mine?'
Wife: 'Those they gave away.'
Husband: 'I had a dream too. I dreamt they were auctioning off pussies. The pretty ones went for a thousand dollars, and the little tight ones went for two thousand.'
Wife: 'And how much for the ones like mine?'
Husband: 'That's where they held the auction!'

AUSSIE BLOKES

Nicknames: Bazza, Butch, Digger, Browneye, Tiger, Spaz, Sparkie, Flagons, Keeno, Turd, Taz, Nipper, Bonza, True Blue, Pie, Weldo, Fang, Cyril, Teddy, Blacky, Tazzy, Little Roo, Harpo, Dogga, The Judge, Kanga, Tit, Roadrunner, Wally Wombat, Knackers, Boof, Daffy Duck, Spaz, Face, Wank, Choco, Crosseyed Chris, Loey the Legend, Sponge, Nickabocka, Woody, Bomber, Ned Kelly, Mongrel, Waldo, Stevo, Jacko, Sparrow, Steamin' Demon, Choofa, Kicky, Super Charge, Plugger, Woodsman, Tugga.

AVIATION

Jerry walked into the senior pilot's office shaking his head. 'I knew it,' he mumbled.

'What, Jerry?' asked the chief.

'I knew that the propellor on a plane was just for keeping the pilot cool?'

'What do you mean?'

'I was just flying back from Lilydale when the motor coughed, spluttered and died. Then the prop stopped. I tell you I really started to sweat. There's one good thing about having two propellors when you fly.'

'Why's that?' asked the chief.

'Well, if one motor stops, at least the other prop can take you to the scene of the accident!'

The photographer for a national magazine was assigned to get photos of a bushfire. Smoke at the scene was too thick to get any good shots, so he frantically called his home office to hire a plane.

'It will be waiting for you at the airport!' he was assured by his editor.

Sure enough, when he got to the small country airport, there was the plane warming up on the runway. He jumped in with his equipment and yelled, 'Let's go! Let's go!'

The pilot swung the plane into the wind and soon they were up in the air.

'Fly over the north side of the fire,' said the photographer, 'and make three or four low level passes.'

'Why?' asked the pilot.

'Because I'm going to take pictures! I'm a photographer, and photographers take pictures!' said the photographer, by now totally exasperated and impatient.

After a long pause the pilot said, 'You mean you're not the instructor?'

FROM AIRLINE MAINTENANCE LOGBOOKS

Problem: Something loose in cockpit.
Solution: Something tightened in cockpit.

Problem: Evidence of hydraulic leak on right main landing gear.
Solution: Evidence removed.

Problem: DME volume unbelievably loud.
Solution: Volume set to more believable level.

Problem: Dead bugs on windshield.
Solution: Live bugs on order.

Problem: Autopilot in altitude hold mode produces a 200 fpm descent.
Solution: Cannot reproduce problem on ground.

Problem: IFF inoperative.
Solution: IFF inoperative in OFF mode.

Problem: Friction locks cause throttle levers to stick.
Solution: That's what they're there for.

Problem: Number three engine missing.
Solution: Engine found on right wing after brief search.

A man is flying in a hot air balloon and realises he is lost. He reduces height and spots someone below.

He lowers the balloon further and shouts, 'Excuse me, can you tell me where I am?'

The man below says, 'Yes, you're in a hot air

balloon, hovering 15 metres above this field.'

'You must work in tech support,' says the balloonist.

'I do,' replies the man. 'How did you know?'

'Well,' says the balloonist, 'Everything you have told me is technically correct, but it's no use to anyone.'

The man below says, 'You must work in management.'

'I do,' replies the balloonist, 'But how did you know?'

'Well', says the man, 'You don't know where you are, or where you're going, but you expect me to be able to help. You're in the same position you were before we met, but now it's my fault.'

B

BABY

It was the stir of the town when an 80-year-old man married a 20-year-old girl. After a year she went into the hospital to give birth. The nurse came out to congratulate the fellow saying, 'This is amazing. How do you do it at your age?'

He answered, 'You've got to keep that old motor running.'

The following year his wife gave birth again. The same nurse said, 'You really are amazing. How do you do it?'

Again he said, 'You've got to keep the old motor running.'

The same thing happened the next year. The nurse said, 'You must be quite a man.' He responded as usual, 'You've got to keep that old motor running.'

The nurse then said, 'Well, you had better change the oil. This one's black.'

BACHELORS

Two confirmed bachelors sat talking, their conversation drifted to cooking.

'I got a cookbook once,' said one, 'But I could never do anything with it.'

'Too much fancy work in it, eh?' asked the other.

'You said it. Every one of the recipes began the same way: "Take a clean dish ..."'

BAKED BEANS

A man had a full can of baked beans for lunch and by the time he got home his guts were rumbling. He knew he'd have to watch he didn't fart in front of his lovely new wife. His wife, pleased to see him, exclaimed, 'I have a wonderful surprise for dinner tonight.'

She blindfolded him and led him to a chair at the end of the diningroom table. He at down and just as she was ready to remove the blindfold, the phone rang. Making him promise not to remove the blindfold until she returned, she went to answer the phone. He could hear her in the hallway, so wasn't worried about farting and talking out loud to himself. Seizing the opportunity, he shifted his weight onto one leg and let go, loudly, and as ripe as rotten eggs.

'Jesus that will turn the fucking chooks into randy roosters.' He shifted his weight onto the other leg and let go again. 'Well fuck me, I think I've shit myself,' he declared. He laughed aloud.

He was smiling contentedly to himself when his wife returned.

With some ceremony, she removed the blindfold. There was his dinner surprise — his stunned parents-in-law and eight other guests, seated around the table for his surprise birthday dinner!

BALDNESS

You reach a certain age when your hair stops growing out of your head.
It grows out of your ears and nose instead.

BALLERINA

This woman is sitting in a bar, wearing some sort of tube top. She has never shaved her armpits in her entire life so, as a result, she has a thick black bush under each arm. Every 20 minutes, she raises her arm up and flags the bartender for another drink. This goes on all night so the other people in the bar see her hairy pits every time she raises her arm.

Near the end of the night, this drunk at the end of the bar says to the bartender, 'Hey, I'd like to buy the ballerina a drink.'

The bartender replies, 'She's not a ballerina. What makes you think she's a ballerina?'

The drunk says, 'Any girl that can lift her leg that high *has* to be a ballerina!'

BALLS!

A drunk was in the bar of the Royal in Bundaberg. He gets up from the bar and heads for the bathroom. A few minutes later, a blood-curdling scream is heard from the dunny. Then another loud scream reverberates through the bar.

The bartender rushes into the dunny to investigate.

'What's all the screaming about in there?' he yells. 'You're scaring my customers!'

'I'm just sitting here on the toilet,' slurs the

drunk, 'And every time I try to flush, something comes up and squeezes the hell out of my balls.'

The bartender opens the door, looks in, and says, 'You idiot! You're sitting on the mop bucket!'

Women rub their eyes when they get up in the morning because they have no balls to scratch.

The National Institute of Scientific Investigation has announced the results of their two-year research into corporate Australia's recreation preferences.

The sport of choice for unemployed or incarcerated people is: BASKETBALL.

The sport of choice for maintenance-level employees is: BOWLING.

The sport of choice for front-line workers is: FOOTBALL.

The sport of choice for supervisors is: BASEBALL.

The sport of choice for middle management is: TENNIS.

The sport of choice for senior executives is: GOLF.

Conclusion: The higher you are in the corporate structure, the smaller your balls.

A man travels to Spain and goes to a Madrid restaurant for a late dinner. He orders the house special and he is brought a plate with potatoes, corn and two large meaty objects.
'What's this?' he asks the waiter.
'Cojones, senor,' the waiter replies.
'What are cojones?' the man asks.
'Cojones,' the waiter explains, 'are the testicles of the bull who lost at the arena this afternoon.'
At first the man is disgusted, but being the adven-

turous type, he decides to try this local delicacy. To his amazement, it is quite delicious, and it is so nice that the man decides to come back the next night and order it again. This time, the waiter brings out the plate, but the meaty objects are much smaller.

'What's this?' the man asks the waiter.

'Cojones, senor,' replies the waiter.

'No, no,' the man objects, 'I had cojones last night and they were much bigger than these!'

'Senor,' the waiter explains, 'the bull does not always lose!'

BASTARDS

Once not too long ago in Ireland there lived a family made up of a mother, father, and three boys. The family lived on a farm and all were big, husky people except, that is, for the youngest boy who was small and skinny.

Days past and turned into years, then one day the father fell sick. Things turned from bad to worse, and worse yet, until soon he was lying on his death bed.

Now it's an old Irish tradition to be able to ask one question, anything at all, on your death bed, and it must be answered truthfully. So with all the family round him, he mustered up the strength to call his wife to him. She leant down so she could hear his faint voice.

'I'm going to ask you a question,' he said to his wife.

'All right, ask me what you will, and I shall answer you true,' she said, holding his feeble hand.

The man took in a deep breath and motioned as he spoke, 'The boy there, on the end of the bed, the skinny one, is he mine?'

The mother sat looking at the skinny, feeble boy for a moment, then turning back to her dying husband she said, 'Yes, he's yours, for sure he is.'

With that, the old man died with a smile on his face.

The mother folded his hands across his dead body, stood up, looked at her sons, and said, 'I'm glad he didn't ask about you other two!'

BEER

How many men does it take to open a beer?
None. She should open it before she brings it to the couch.

How is being at a singles bar different from going to the circus?
At the circus the clowns don't talk.

He is a wise man who invented beer.
— Plato, Greek philosopher

I've got Aids — Alcohol Induced Dizzy Spells.
— sign on rear window of red Falcon ute, Geelong

Always do sober what said you'd do drunk.
That will teach you to keep your mouth shut.
— Ernest Hemingway, writer and drunk

I don't drink water. Fish fuck in it.
— Oscar Fingal O'Flahertie Wills Wilde (1854–1900),
Irish dramatist, poet, novelist, essayist, critic

A woman drove me to drink,
And I never had the courtesy to thank her.
— W. C. Fields, actor

Beer makes you feel the way you ought to feel without beer.
— Henry Lawson (1867–1922)
The first articulate voice of Australia, swagman, poet, writer, genius, drunk

You're not drunk if you can lie on the floor without holding on.
— Dean Martin, singer, actor

Give me a women who loves beer and I will conquer the world.
— Kaiser Wilhelm

There can't be good living where there is not good drinking.
— Benjamin Franklin (1706-90)
American statesman, diplomat, author, scientist, inventor

There is a police car parked outside a nightclub in Perth one Friday night, at closing time. The first patron out of the door staggers to a nearby car and tries to unlock the door with his keys. Unable to open the door, he tries another car, again with no success. He then staggers across the parking lot to his own car, and sits down inside.

Meanwhile, the other bar patrons file quietly to their cars. The first guy out starts waving and singing and saying goodnight to the other patrons. Finally, after all the other patrons had left, he gets in his car, starts it up. Before he even gets the car in gear, the policeman turns on his lights and pulls up beside him. The officer says, 'Get out of your car, I'm giving you a breathalyser.'

The patron agrees, and blows into the testing device. The officer checks the reading, and it is 0.0. The patron says that he had not been drinking at all that evening. Confused, the officer asks why he was staggering through the parking lot, seemingly inebriated.

The patron says simply, 'I'm the designated distraction.'

BEER DRINKING PROBLEMS

Symptom: Feet cold and wet.
Fault: Glass being held at incorrect angle.
Action: Rotate glass so that the open end points toward ceiling.

Symptom: Feet warm and wet.
Fault: Improper bladder control.
Action: Stand next to the nearest dog and complain about house training.

Symptom: Beer unusually pale and tasteless.
Fault: Glass empty.
Action: Get someone to buy you another beer.

Symptom: Opposite wall covered with fluorescent lights.
Fault: You have fallen over backwards.
Action: Have yourself leashed to the bar.

Symptom: Mouth contains cigarette butts.
Fault: You have fallen forward.
Action: See above.

Symptom: Beer tasteless and the front end of your shirt is wet.
Fault: Mouth not open or glass applied to the wrong face.
Action: Retire to the restroom and practise in the mirror.

Symptom: Floor blurred.
Fault: You are looking through an empty glass.
Action: Get someone to buy you another beer.

Symptom: Floor moving.
Fault: You are being carried out.
Action: Find out if you are being taken to another bar.

Symptom: Room seems unusually dark.
Fault: Bar has closed.
Action: Confirm home address with the baman.

Symptom: Taxi suddenly takes on colourful aspects and textures.
Fault: Beer consumption has exceeded personal limitations.
Action: Cover mouth.

Symptom: Everyone looks up to you and smiles.
Fault: You're dancing on the table.
Action: Fall on someone cushy-looking.

Symptom: Beer is crystal clear.
Fault: Someone is trying to sober you up.
Action: Punch him.

Symptom: Hands hurt, nose hurts, mind unusually clear.
Fault: You have been in a fight.
Action: Apologise to everyone you see, just in case it was them.

Symptom: Don't recognise anyone, don't recognise the room you're in.
Fault: You've wandered into the wrong party.
Action: See if they have free beer.

Symptom: Your singing sounds distorted.
Fault: The beer is too weak.
Action: Have more beer until your voice improves.

Symptom: Don't remember the words to the song.
Fault: Beer is just right.
Action: Play air guitar.

BEER LABELS

Beer drinkers may soon have to put up with the following warnings on their favourite beer labels:

WARNING: Consumption of alcohol may make you think you are whispering when you are not.

WARNING: Consumption of alcohol is a major factor in dancing like a wanker.

WARNING: Consumption of alcohol may make you tell the same boring story over and over until your friends want to smash your head in.

WARNING: Consumption of alcohol may cause you to thay shings like thish.

WARNING: Consumption of alcohol may lead you to believe that ex-lovers are dying for you to telephone them at four in the morning.

WARNING: Consumption of alcohol may leave you wondering what the hell happened to your trousers.

WARNING: Consumption of alcohol may make you think you can converse logically with members of the opposite sex without spitting.

WARNING: Consumption of alcohol may make you think you have mystical karate powers.

WARNING: Consumption of alcohol may cause you to roll over in the morning and see something really scary (whose name you can't remember).

WARNING: Consumption of alcohol is the leading cause of inexplicable rug burns on the forehead.

WARNING: Consumption of alcohol may lead to traffic signs and cones appearing in your home.

WARNING: Consumption of alcohol may create the illusion that you are tougher, handsomer and smarter than some really, really big blokes with muscles.

WARNING: Consumption of alcohol may lead you to believe you are invisible.

WARNING: Consumption of alcohol may lead you to believe people are laughing *with* you.

WARNING: Consumption of alcohol may actually *cause* pregnancy.

BELLY BUTTONS

People have belly buttons to hold your chewing gum while on the way down.

The pretty coed nervously asked the doctor to perform an unusual operation, removing a large chunk of green wax from her navel.

Looking up from the ticklish task, the doctor asked, 'How did this happen?'

'Let me put it this way, doc,' the girl began, 'My boyfriend likes to eat by candlelight.'

BIG FART

Bill and Jim were a couple of drinking mates who worked as airplane mechanics in Sydney. One day the airport was fogged in and they stuck in the hangar with nothing to do. Bill said, 'Mate, I wish we had something to drink!'

Jim says, 'Me too. Y'know, I've heard you can drink jet fuel and get a buzz. You wanna try it?'

So they pour themselves a couple of glasses of high octane fuel and get completely smashed. The next morning Bill wakes up and is surprised at how good he feels. In fact he feels GREAT! NO hangover! NO bad side effects. Nothing!

Then the phone rings. It's Jim.

Jim says, 'Hey, how do you feel this morning?'

Bill says, 'I feel great. How about you?'

Jim says, 'I feel great, too. You don't have a hangover?'

Bill says, 'No, that jet fuel is great stuff — no hangover, nothing. We ought to do this more often.'

'Yeah, well there's just one thing...'

'What's that?'

'Have you farted yet?'

'No...'

'Well, DON'T, ... I ended up in MELBOURNE!'

BIKE RIDE

A man decided that he was going to ride a 10-speed bike from Sydney to Dubbo. He got as far as the

Blue Mountains before the mountains just became too much and he could go no farther. He stuck his thumb out, but after three hours hadn't had a single car stop. At last a bloke in a hot HSV Holden pulled over and offered him a ride.

Of course, the bike wouldn't fit in the car, so the driver found a piece of rope in his boot and tied it to the bumper. He tied the other end to the bike and told the man that, if he was going too fast, he should ring the bell on his handlebars and he would slow down.

Everything went fine for the first 30 miles. Then a XR8 Falcon blew past them. Not to be outdone, the Holden pulling the bike took off after the other car. A short distance down the road, the two cars, both going well over 140 k.p.h., blew through a speed trap. The police officer noted the speeds from his radar gun and radioed ahead to the next police car that he had two cars headed his way at over 140 k.p.h.,

'... and you're not going to believe this, but there's guy on a 10-speed bike ringing his bell trying to get past.'

BLOKES

BLOKE: Australian colloq. Man. Male of the species. (A legend in his own mind, created by God in his own image, to rule the world. Perhaps one of God's few mistakes.)
Man, men (pl.), fellow, fella, cobber, guy, buddy,

bastard, Him, It, the old man, Uncle, Boss, Son, Dad, Gramps, Grandpa, Pa, Pop, root rat, humper, chick magnet, ladies man, stud, sex on legs, mate, china plate, hoon, wally, bodgie, drongo, fuckwit, dork, wank, wanker, fartbag, fart machine, old fart, son-of-a-bitch, mother fucker, pisshead, piss pot, prick, dickhead, penis head, shit-head, thick as bricks, homosexual, gay, cocksucker, fairy, nancy boy, pansy, poofter, poo-jammer, poo-pusher, tail-gunner, whoosh, girlieboy, chick with dick.

How can you tell Colonel Sanders was a typical male?
All he cared about were legs, breasts and thighs.

BLONDES

A blonde has been working in a broom factory since childhood. But one day, she storms into the manager's office and exclaims, 'I quit this job, I'm not working here anymore.' The manager naturally doesn't want to lose a hardworking and beautiful girl, so he calms her down and asks what the problem is. After a lot of cajoling, she finally tells him. 'I've been working here so long with the bristles that I've grown them between my legs.'

At this the manager laughs and tells her that it's a common thing and happens to everyone as they grow older. But she does not believe him, so finally he locks the door and tells her, 'Look, I'll prove it to you. I'll drop my pants and you can see that I've grown them too.' So he strips in front of her.

At this, the blonde cries out, 'Oh my God! It's worse than I thought. You've grown the broom handle as well.'

There were three women who were at the gynaecologist having pre-natal checkups. The doctor asked the first woman, 'In what position was the baby conceived?' 'He was on top,' she replied. 'You will have a boy!' the doctor exclaimed. The second woman was asked the same question. 'I was on top,' was the reply. 'You will have a baby girl,' said the doctor. With this, the third women, a blonde, burst into tears. 'What's the matter?' asked the doc. 'Am I going to have puppies?'

A blonde is suffering from a sore throat so she goes to see the doctor. She explains the problem to the doctor who asks her to sit down. He gets out his torch and says, 'Open wide.' 'I can't,' replies the blonde, 'the chair's fitted with arms.'

After many hours of extremely acrobatic and exhausting sex with a blonde he had just picked up, a man goes into the kitchen for some food to replenish his just-spent energy. He pours himself a glass of milk and right before drinking it, he realises his manhood is still pretty hot, so he sticks it in the glass to cool it off. Just then the blonde walks in and says, 'Oh, I always wondered how you refilled those.'

This blonde is so dumb — She doesn't realise that you can play the AM radio in the afternoon.

There are three women working in the same office: a brunette, a redhead and a blonde. They begin to notice that each day the boss, who is also a woman, leaves work early.

One day they decide that once the boss takes off, they will leave right after her. So they all three leave. The brunette goes to visit her mother. The redhead goes shopping. The blonde was just happy to get home early. She hears a noise from her bedroom, so sneaks upstairs and opens the door a little. She is horrified to see her husband in bed with HER BOSS! She closes the door and leaves.

Next day the brunette asks if they are going to sneak off again today?

'NO WAY!' says the blonde, 'I nearly got caught yesterday!'

A pregnant woman walked into a doctor's office to have an ultrasound. The doctor told her that she was going to have a little girl and asked what she would call her.

She said, 'Barbara.'

He then asked her, 'Do you have any other children?'

She said, 'Five other daughters, and their names are also Barbara.'

Puzzled, the doctor asked, 'How do you call them all home for dinner?'

She replied, 'That's easy I just yell, "Barbara! Supper!" and they all come home.'

He then asked, 'What if you're going somewhere?'

She said, 'That's easy too. I just say, "Barbara, let's go!" and they all come running.'

He questioned her again, 'What if you only want to speak to one of them?'

'Well, then I just call them by their last name.'

Why can't blondes waterski?
Because when their crotches get wet they want to lie down.

A young couple got married and left on their honeymoon. When they got back, the bride immediately called her mother.

'Well,' said her mother, 'So, how was the honeymoon?'

'Oh, mama,' she replied, 'The honeymoon was wonderful! So romantic ...' Then she burst out crying. 'But, mama, as soon as we returned Sam started using the most horrible language — things I'd never heard before! I mean, all these awful four-letter words! You've got to come and take me home ... PLEASE, MAMA!'

'Sarah, Sarah,' her mother said, 'Calm down! Tell me, what could be so awful? WHAT four-letter words?'

'Please don't make me tell you, mama,' wept the daughter, 'I'm so embarrassed — they're just too awful! COME AND GET ME, PLEASE!'

'Darling, baby, you must tell me what has you so

upset ... Tell your mother these horrible four-letter words!'

Still sobbing, the bride said, 'Oh, mama ... words like ... Dust, Wash, Iron, Cook.'

A blonde decides one day that she is sick and tired of all these blonde jokes, and of how all blondes are perceived as stupid. She decides to show her husband that blondes really are smart. While her husband is at work, she decides that she is going to paint a couple of rooms in the house.

Next day, right after her husband leaves for work, she gets down to the task at hand. Her husband arrives home at 5.30 and smells the distinctive smell of paint. He walks into the living room and finds his wife lying on the floor in a pool of sweat. He notices that she is wearing a ski jacket and a fur coat at the same time. He rushes over and says, 'Gees, are you all right?'

She slowly nods her head.

'What are you doing?' he asks incredulously.

'I wanted to prove that not all blonde women are dumb,' she starts, 'And I wanted to do it by painting the house.'

'Well, why do you have both a ski jacket and a fur coat on?' he asks dumbfounded.

'Well,' she says, 'I was reading the directions on the tin and it said: "For best results, put on two coats."'

How did the blonde break her arm while she was raking leaves?
She fell out of the tree.

There was a group of people in an Adelaide office standing around talking about how stupid blondes are. There was a blonde female in the group and she was really offended. She told them that they were being unfair; she was really smart, and blonde too. So they asked her if she knew all the states and capitals. She said, 'Yes, of course.' So then they asked her what the capital of Queensland was. Without hesitation, the blonde said, 'Q'.

What did the blonde say when asked if she'd been picked up by the fuzz?
No … but I've been swung around by the tits.

BLOWJOB

A guy with a severe case of laryngitis goes into a pub and asks the barman for a whisky. The barman says, 'You sound horrible, what's the problem?'
  'I've had this terrible case of laryngitis for two weeks and it just won't get any better.'
  'I know just what you mean,' says the barman. 'I had the same thing a month ago.'
  'How did you get rid of it,' says the bloke.

'I got the wife to give me a twenty-minute blowjob and it was gone the next day,' says the barman.
'Is your wife home now,' says the patron?

What's the best thing about a blowjob?
The ten minutes of silence.

BMW

Why do South Australians like BMWs?
It's a word they can spell.

BOMBER

Did you hear about the South Australian terrorist who tried to blow up a school bus?
He burnt his lips on the exhaust pipe.

BOSS

A boss was sticking it up one of his employees in front of the entire office. When the embarrassed youth was told in a snide manner, 'That's not quite the answer I wanted,' the young man, who had had enough, retorted: 'Then don't ask the fucking question!'

BOXING

Ralph was in the gym at Goulburn, NSW, for his first workout. He wanted desperately to prove he had the makings of a great boxer, so made sure he threw everything at his opponent. By round three he still hadn't hit the more experienced boxer, but he knew he was doing his best. He kept swinging punches but only raised fresh air. When he asked his trainer between rounds how he was doing, the trainer looked at him and drily said, 'Keep it up. At this rate with a bit of luck he'll feel the draughts and catch a cold.'

BRAS

A man walks into the woman's section of a department store and tells the sales clerk he wants to buy a bra for his wife.

'What type of bra?' asks the clerk.

'Type?' inquires the man. 'Are there more than one type?'

'There are three types,' replies the clerk. 'The Catholic type, the Salvation Army type, and the Baptist type.'

Still confused, the man asks, 'What is the difference?'

The clerk replies, 'It is really very easy. The Catholic type supports the masses; the Salvation Army type lifts up the fallen; and the Baptist type makes mountains out of mole hills.'

BREASTS

It's a warm summer night in Brisbane and a man and wife are in their bedroom. The wife is looking at her naked body in the full-length mirror with a frown on her face.

'What's the matter, dear?' the man asks.

'Oh, I was just looking at my breasts. I wish there was some way to make them grow larger,' she sighs.

'Well why don't you just wrap your hand in toilet paper and rub it between your tits every day.'

Puzzled, the wife asks, 'Do you really think that that'll help?'

With a smirk, the husband replied, 'Well, look what it did for your arse!'

A girl is feeling a bit down in the dumps and decides to treat herself to a meal at the Ritz. She manages to get a table that very night and enjoys a delicious meal on her own, nothing too extravagant, but nice all the same.

When the head waiter brings the bill, she's horrified to see the total: $150.

She didn't expect this at all and asks the waiter, 'Would you mind holding my breasts while I write the cheque please?'

The head waiter is taken aback. In all his years in the job he's never had such a request. Always eager to please the customer, he obliges.

She gets up to leave and the waiter is still perplexed. His curiosity gets the better of him and he catches up with her at the door.

'I'm sorry to bother you, Miss, but I'd like to know why you asked me to do that just now.'

'Oh, it's quite simple really,' she replies. 'I love to have my breasts held when I'm being screwed!'

BRIDGE

A waitress is applying for a new job. She is asked why she left her last job. 'It was in a ridiculous club where they played a game called bridge. Last night when I was bringing in refreshments I heard a man say, "Lay down, and let's see what you've got." Another said, "I got strength, but no length." The next man says to a lady, "Take your hand off my trick." Next a lady says, "You forced me! You jumped me twice when you didn't have the strength for one raise!" Another lady is talking about protecting her honour, then says, "Now it's time for me to play with your husband and you can play with mine." I decided to quit, and just as I'm leaving I heard one of them say, "I guess we'll have to go home now. This is the last rubber!"

BROTHER

'Gees, I'll be glad when I get a little brother,' says young Michael. 'There's only so much you get away with by blaming it on the dog.'

BUMMER!

- 💀 Men are more likely to be hanged.
- 💀 Men normally don't live a long as women.
- 💀 Men get scrotum rash.
- 💀 Men find it hard to undo bras.

BUT BEWDIE!

Men's dangling bits don't attract as much attention as women's bouncy bits.

Men are more likely to know how to fit a 9-inch diff.

Men never have to wear a bra.

BUMPER STICKERS

Who lit the fuse on your tampon?

I don't have a licence to kill. I have a learner's permit.

I wasn't born a bitch. Men like you made me this way.

If you can read this, I can hit my brakes and sue you.

Lose your cat? Check my tyres.

Don't drink and drive. You might hit a bump and spill your drink.

My kid beat the crap out of your honour student.

Reality is for the people who can't handle the drugs.

If you can read this, I've lost my caravan.

Support cannibalism — EAT ME!

Five days a week my body is a temple. The other two, it's an amusement park.

If we are what we eat, I'm cheap, fast and easy.

My wife keeps complaining I never listen to her ... or something like that.

EARTH FIRST! We'll strip-mine the other planets later.

If you drink, don't park.
Accidents cause people.

God is my co-pilot, but the
Devil is my bombardier.

Stop repeat offenders.
Don't re-elect them!

BURGLER

Late one night, a burglar broke into a house that he thought was empty. He tiptoed through the living room but he froze in his tracks when he heard a loud voice say, 'Jesus is watching you!'

Terrified, he looked all around. In a dark corner, he spotted a bird cage with a parrot in it. He asked the parrot, 'Was that you who said Jesus is watching me?'

'Yes,' said the parrot.

The burglar breathed a sigh of relief, then he asked the parrot, 'What's your name?'

'Clarence,' said the bird.

'That's a dumb name for a parrot,' sneered the burglar. 'What idiot named you Clarence?'

The parrot said, 'The same idiot who named the Rottweiler Jesus.'

BUTCHER'S MEAT

It had been many years since that embarrassing day when a young woman, baby in arm, had entered the butcher shop and confronted its owner with the news that the baby was his, and what was he going to do about it? He had offered to give her free meat until the boy was 16. She agreed.

The man had been counting off the years on his calendar until one day, the teenager, who had been coming to collect the meat each week, boasted to the butcher, 'I'll be 16 tomorrow.'

'I know,' said the butcher with a smile. 'I've been waiting for this day a long time. Tell your mother, when you take this parcel of meat home, that it's the last free meat she'll get. Watch the expression on her face.'

The boy took the meat home and told his mother what the butcher had said. Mother nodded and said, 'Son, go back to the butcher and tell him I have also had free bread, free milk, and free groceries for the last 16 years … and watch the expression on his face!'

BUTLER

A wealthy couple had plans to go to an evening ball. So they told their butler that they were giving him the evening off to do as he pleased since they would be out until quite late.

The couple went to the ball and dinner. After an

hour and a half, the wife told her husband that she was horribly bored and that she would prefer to go home and finish some work for the next day. The husband had to stay for a few more hours to meet some very important people so the wife went home alone and found the butler spread out on the couch watching TV.

She slowly moved towards him and sat down very seductively. She then told him to come closer. Then even closer. She moved forward and whispered in his ear, 'Take off my dress.'

'Now take off my bra.

'Next remove my shoes and stockings.

'Now remove my garter belt and panties.'

She then looked deep into his eyes and in a sharp voice shouted, 'The next time I catch you wearing my clothes, you're fired.'

C

CARS IN HEAVEN

Once there were three men, Dave, John, and Sam, who were involved in a tragic car accident in which all three died. As they stood at the gates of heaven St Peter came up to them and said, 'You will all be given a method of transportation for your eternal use around heaven. You will be judged on your past deeds, and will have your transport chosen accordingly.' St Peter looked at Dave and said, 'You, Dave, were a bad man. You cheated on your wife four times! For this, you will drive around Heaven in an old beat up Holden.'

Next St Peter looked at John and said, 'You were not so evil, but you still cheated on your wife twice. For this, you will forever travel around heaven in a Ford.

St Peter finally looked at Sam, and said, 'You, Sam, have set a fine example. You did not have sex until after marriage, and you never cheated on your wife! For this, you will forever travel through heaven in a Rolls.'

A short time later Jon and Dave pulled up in their cars next to Sam's Rolls and there he is, sitting on the hood, head in hands, crying.

'What's wrong, Sam?' they asked. 'You got the Rolls! You are set forever! Why so down?'

Sam looked up, ever so slowly opened his mouth, and cried, 'I just saw my wife go by on a skate board.'

CAT IN HEAVEN

One day a cat dies of natural causes and goes to heaven. There he meets the Lord himself. The Lord says to the cat, 'You lived a good life and if there is any way I can make your stay in Heaven more comfortable, please let me know.'

The cat thinks for a moment and says, 'Lord, all my life I have lived with a poor family and had to sleep on a hard wooden floor.' The Lord stops the cat and says, 'Say no more,' and a wonderful fluffy pillow appears.

A few days later six mice are killed in a tragic farming accident and go to heaven. The Lord greets them with the same offer. The mice answer, 'All of our lives we have been chased. We have had to run from cats, dogs and even women with brooms. Running, running, running ... we're tired of running. Do you think we could have roller skates so we don't have to run any more?' The Lord says, 'Say no more,' and fits each mouse with beautiful new roller skates.

About a week later the Lord stops by to see the cat and finds him snoozing on the pillow. The Lord gently wakes the cat and asks, 'How are things since you got here?'

The cat stretches, yawns and replies, 'It is wonderful here. Better than I could have ever expected. And those "Meals On Wheels" you've been sending by are the best!'

CATCH!

A man in New South Wales died from snake bite. Big deal you may say, but this was snake bite with a difference. It seems he and a friend were playing catch with a snake. You can guess what happened. The friend was hospitalised.

CATHOLIC BISHOP & CHOIRBOY

The local bishop was having anal intercourse with a choir boy in the back seats of St Mary's. He was so preoccupied that he didn't hear a tourist approach him. But the flash of the camera brought him back to earth with a jolt.

'Please, please, sell me the film,' he begged. 'In fact, I'll buy the camera.'

Later the dean noticed that the bishop had a new camera.

'How much did you pay for it?'

The bishop said, very glumly, 'One thousand dollars.'

'Christ,' said the dean, 'Somebody saw you coming!'

CATHOLIC RABBI

There was a rabbi who went to the Catholic priest at the church and asked, 'How do you get the money to make your church so beautiful?'

The priest said, 'We hear confessions; observe while I demonstrate.' So the priest gets in the centre compartment, the rabbi on one side, and in walks the first penitent.

'It's been one week since my last confession and I have committed adultery three times.'

The priest says, 'For your penance say a Hail Mary and put five dollars in the collection box and your sins will be forgiven.'

The next penitent walks in and says, 'It's been one week since my last confession and I've committed adultery three times.'

The priest says, 'For your penance say a Hail Mary and put five dollars in the collection box and your sins will be forgiven.'

The rabbi says, 'Ooh, can I try?' So the priest and the rabbi switch booths. In walks the next penitent. 'Can I help you,' says the rabbi.

The penitent says, 'It's been one week since my last confession and I've committed adultery twice.'

The rabbi says, 'Go out and do it a third time; we have a special — three for five dollars!'

CATHOLIC SCHOOL

A kid is failing all his exams at a public school, so his parents move him into a private catholic school. All the sudden his grades skyrocket up to As. Then one night at the dinner table his parents ask, 'Why were you doing so badly in a public school, and when we switched you to a private catholic school you did so well?'

The kid responds, 'Because I knew they were serious about punishment if you didn't work hard. The first day I walked in and there's the bloke nailed to a plus sign.'

CATHOLIC v. PROTESTANT

Sister Catherine was asking all the Catholic school children in fourth grade what they want to be when they grow up. Little Sheila said, 'When I grow up, I want to be a prostitute!'

Sister Catherine's eyes grew wide and she barked, 'What did you say?'

'A prostitute!' Sheila exclaimed.

Sister Catherine breathed a sight of relief and said,

'Whew! Praise the Lord! For a moment I thought you said "A protestant"!'

The pope and Queen Elizabeth were standing on a balcony beaming at thousands of people in the forecourt below. The queen says to the pope out of the corner of her mouth, 'I bet you a tenner that I can make every English protestant person in the crowd go wild with just a wave of my hand.'

The pope says, 'No way. You can't do that.'

The queen says, 'Watch this,' and she waves her hand. Every English person in the crowd goes crazy, waving their little plastic Union Jacks on sticks and cheering, basically going ballistic.

The pope thinks to himself for a minute and then he turns to her and says, 'I bet you I can make every Irish catholic and protestant person in the crowd go wild, with just one nod of my head.'

The queen says, 'No way, it can't be done.'

So the pope headbutts her.

CAVE MEN

Why did cavemen drag their women around by the hair?
Because if they did it by the legs the women would fill up.

CELIBACY

Barney and Jim were having a beer at the Royal.

'You know, I went twelve years without sex. I was totally celibate,' said Barney.

'Christ, how come? Were your bothered by it?'
'Nah, mate, not a bit. 'Cause then I had my thirteenth birthday, ha-ha!'

CHAPPED LIPS

Two church-going women were gossiping in front of the country store when a dusty old drover rode up. He tied up in front of the pub, walked around behind his horse, lifted its tail and kissed the horse full on its arsehole.

Repulsed, one of the women asked, 'That's disgusting, why did you do that?' To which the drover replied, 'I've got chapped lips.'

Confused, the woman continued, 'Does that make them feel better?'

'No, but it stops me from licking them!'

CHICKEN MAN

A man was driving along a rural road when he remembered he had to make a phone call. He was miles from a pay phone so he decided to stop in at the next house he found. As he was approaching the house he noticed a three-legged chicken racing along the road. He followed the chicken and clocked it at 90 kilometres per hour.

When the man got to the house he asked the farmer about the chicken. The farmer replied,

'When I was at the uneeversitee I studied geenetics. We love chicken and we're all partial to a drumstick, so I thought I'd see if I could make a three-legged chicken. So, there it is.'

The man was quite impressed. He asked, 'How does it taste?'

The farmer replied, 'Don't know. None of us have been able to catch one yet.'

CHINESE DICTIONARY

Dung On Mai Shu — I stepped in excrement.
Ai Wan Tu Bang Yu — Let's sleep together.
Ai Bang Mai Ne — I bumped into the coffee table.
Fat Ho — An unattractive woman.
Ar U Wun Tu — A gay liberation greeting.
Chin Tu Fat — You need a face lift.
Chow Mai Dong — Blow me.

Dum Gai — A stupid person.
Wel Hung Gai — Is that a banana in your pocket?
Won Hung Low — Southern Chinese dialect for Wel Hung Gai.
Gun Pao Der — An ancient Chinese invention.
Hu Flung Dung — Which one of you fertilised the field?
Hu Yu Hai Ding — We have reason to believe you are harbouring a fugitive.
Hum Hia — Approach me.
Lao Ze Sho — Gilligan's Island.
Lao Zi — Not very good.
Shai Gai — A bashful person.
Tai Ne Bae Be — A premature infant.
Tai Ne Po Ne — A small horse.
Ten Ding Ba — Serving drinks to people.
Wan Bum Lung — A person with TB.
Yu Mai Te Tan — Your holiday on the Gold Coast agreed with you.
Wa Shing Kah — Cleaning the car.
Wai So Dim — Are you trying to save electricity?
Wai U Shao Ting — There is no reason to raise your voice.

CLITORIS

What is a clitoris?
A female hood ornament.

COCK SHOT

A man walks into a gunshop and asks for a sight for his gun. The salesman gets one, fits it to a gun he has nearby and says, 'This is the best I have.'

The man asks, 'How do I know?'

So the man lines it up and says, 'OK, see that house? That's mine, 20 kilometres away.'

The man wanting to buy the sight has a look through and starts laughing.

'What's funny?' asks the man behind the counter.

'There's a naked woman and a man running around inside the house.'

The salesman has another look, and says, 'That's my wife, the cheating bitch!' He grabs two bullets, loads them and says to his customer. 'If you can shoot my wife in the head and the guy in the cock, I'll give you the gun and the sight for free.'

The customer lines it up and says, 'I think I can do this with one shot!'

COCOPOPS

Two little kids, Bill and Ben, decide it's time to learn how to swear. So, Bill says, 'OK, you say "arse" and I'll say "hell".' All excited about their plan, they go to the kitchen where their mother asks them what they'd like for breakfast. 'Aw, hell, gimme some Cocopops,' says Ben.

His mother backhands him off the stool, sending him bawling out of the room, and turns to the brother, 'What'll you have?'

'I dunno,' quavers Bill, 'but you can bet your arse it isn't gonna be Cocopops.'

CODY and THE PREACHER

His real name is Kodey, but I spelt it the way he almost looks — like a Buffalo Bill Cody without a beard. He always wears a large hat. He is a real bush dag and everyone's life of the party. A great story-teller and mate to all. His mate is the Preacher, who turns shy and blushes when Cody tells how he got his name.

'I took him to his first Bachelor and Spinster Ball. He turns up in a black shirt and white bow-tie. Later in the evening I come out and there he is sitting on the tailgate of the ute. A sheila is down on

her knees giving him some head. He's got a look of satisfaction on his face, and he pats her on the head and says, "Bless you my child." And the name of the Preacher has stuck ever since.'

Another yarn he tells anyone in earshot is that everyone wants to stroke his dick. 'Can't go anywhere but they all want to play with my dick, stroke and all that. You want to see my dick?' he asks.

Well, no, not really!

'Oh come on, play with my dick. Here Dick.'

Into the pub walks a beaut black and white border collie.

'There y'are, go play with my Dick, everyone loves my Dick!' as the dog runs amok, tail wagging and saying howdy to everyone.

COME AGAIN?

What is the difference between a woman and a coffin? You come in one and go in the other.

COMMANDER'S COMEUPPANCE

The commanding officer at the army base rang the motor pool. A sleepy voice answered, 'Hullo.'

The CO said, 'How many vehicles in the motor pool?'

The sleepy voice said, 'Hold on.' After a few minutes, he came back on and said, 'There's seven Jeeps, three one and a half tonne trucks, and two staff cars for the fat-arse commanding officer.'

The CO was upset by this and said, 'Do you know who this is?'

Sleepy voice said, 'No.'

The CO yells, 'This is your commanding officer!'

Dead silence for about 5 seconds. Then the sleepy voice asked, 'Do you know who this is?'

The CO says, 'No.'

Sleepy voice replies, 'Good. See ya, fat arse!'

COMPLAINTS

Extracts from a selection of letters of complaint written to the House Commission and Social Security.

Our lavatory seat is broken in half and is now in three pieces.

Can you please tell me when our repairs are going to be done as my wife is about to become an expectant mother?

I want some repairs doing to my cooker as it backfired and burnt my knob off.

The toilet is blocked and we can't bath the children until it is cleared.

Will you please send someone to mend our broken path as my wife tripped and fell on it and she is now pregnant.

Our kitchen floor is very damp and we have two children and we would like a third so will you please send somebody round to do something about it.

Would you please repair our toilet. My son pulled the chain and the box fell on his head.

Mrs Smith has no clothes and has had none for over a year. The clergy have been visiting her.

I need money to buy special medicine for my husband as he is unable.

The man next door has a large erection in his back garden which is unsightly and dangerous.

In reply to your letter, I have already cohabited with your officer with no results so far.

I am pleased to inform you that my husband who was reported missing, is dead.

Mrs Adams has asked me to collect her money as she is going into hospital to have her overtures out.

Sir, I am forwarding my marriage certificate and two children — one of which is a mistake as you will see.

My husband is diabetic and has to take insolence regular but he finds he is lethargic to it.

Unless I get my husband's maintenance money soon I shall be obliged to live an immortal life.

The children have been off school because there is a lot of about and I had them humanised.

Please forward my money at once as I have fallen into errors with my landlord and milkman.

You have changed my little boy into a little girl. Will this matter?

Mrs Brown only THINKS she's ill, but believe me she is nothing but a hypodermic.

In accordance with your instructions I have given birth to twins in the enclosed envelope.

I want my sick pay quick. I have been in bed under the doctor for a week and he is doing me no good. If things don't improve I shall get another doctor.

I do not get any money from my son he is in the army and his regiment is at present manuring on Salisbury plain.

Milk is wanted for my baby and the father is unable to supply it.

Re your dental enquiry. The teeth on top are alright but those on my bottom are hurting dreadfully.

I am very annoyed to find you have branded my son illiterate. This is a lie as I married his father a week before he was born.

This is to let you know there is a smell coming from the man next door.

I am sorry I omitted to put down all my children's names. This was due to contraceptional circumstances.

I wish to complain that my father hurt his ankle very badly when he put his foot in the hole in his back passage.

The lavatory is blocked. This is caused by the boys next door throwing balls on the roof.

COMPUTER TECHNOLOGY FOR TASMANIANS

LOG ON: Making a wood stove hotter.
LOG OFF: Don't add any more wood.
MONITOR: Keeping an eye on the wood stove.
DOWNLOAD: Getting the firewood off the ute.
MEGA HERTZ: When you're not careful getting the firewood.
FLOPPY DISC: What you get from trying to carry too much firewood.
RAM: That thing that splits the firewood.
HARD DRIVE: Getting home in the winter time.
WINDOWS: What to shut when it's cold outside.
SCREEN: What to shut when it's blowie season.
BYTE: What the mozzies do.
MODEM: What you did to the paddock.
DOT MATRIX: Old Dan Matrix's wife.
LAP TOP: Where the cat sleeps.
KEYBOARD: Where you hang the keys.
SOFTWARE: Those plastic forks and knifes.
MOUSE: Eats the wheat in the shed.
MAINFRAME: Holds up the shed.
PORT: Fancy mainland wine
RANDOM ACCESS MEMORY: When you can't remember what you spent at the pub when your wife asks.

CONDOMS

Possible 'tags' if the following companies were to go into the condom market!

Nike Condoms: Just do it.

Toyota Condoms: Oh what a feeling.

Mentos Condoms: The fresh maker.

Macintosh Condom: It does more, it costs less, it's that simple.

Ford Condoms: Have you driven a Ford lately?

Avis Condoms: We try harder.

KFC Condoms: Finger-Licking Good.

Coca-Cola Condoms: The Real Thing.

Bounty Condoms: The quicker picker upper.

Microsoft Condoms:
Where do you want to go today?

Energiser Condoms:
It keeps going and going and going ...

M&M Condoms:
It melts in your mouth, not in your hands!

Delta Airlines Condoms:
Delta is ready when you are.

United Airlines Condoms: Fly United.

The Star Trek Condom:
To Boldly Go Where No Man Has Gone Before.

CONFIDENT BEGGAR

A cold night in a Sydney back street. A young couple are heading for a carpark after a night at the movies. A man looking very much down on his luck approaches.

'Excuse me, good people,' he says as he raises his hat to the lady. 'Could you please show that you have abundant generosity, and assist a poor unfortunate man who has not had the good luck to eat for days, is out of work, with no money, no place to sleep, and no worldly possessions except for this old sawn-off shotgun I have under my coat.'

CONFUCIUS SAYS:

Man who sink into woman's arms will soon have arms in woman's sink.

Letting the cat out of the bag is a whole lot easier than putting it back in.

Good judgement comes from experience, and a lot of that comes from bad judgement.

A good horse never comes in a bad colour.

There are two theories about arguing with a woman. Neither one works.

Don't worry about biting off more than you can chew. Your mouth is probably a whole lot bigger than you think.

If you find yourself in a hole, the first thing to do is stop digging.

Never slap a man who's chewing tobacco.

It don't take a genius to spot a goat in a flock of sheep.

Don't squat with your spurs on.

Always drink upstream from the herd.

When you're throwing your weight around, be ready to have it thrown around by somebody else.

Always take a good look at what you're about to eat. It's not so important to know what it is, but you might need to know what it was.

The quickest way to double your money is to fold it over and put it back in your pocket.

You cannot make a lover out of an ugly wife with money.

From the frying pan of engagement into the fire of matrimony.

A lover in the hand is worth two wives in the bush.

There are three kinds of men:
The one that learns from reading.
The one that learns from observation.
The rest of them have to pee on the electric fence for themselves.

COST PRICE

Customer: 'If these machines are sold way under cost as you claim they are, how do you make a living?'
Salesman: 'Simple, we make our money fixing them.'

CREDIT CRACK

Three guys walk into a strip club and sit at the end of the stage. Almost immediately, a dancer is shaking her arse in the first guy's face. He gives his mates a sly look and pulls $10 out of his pocket, licks it and sticks it to her left cheek. He turns to his mates and says, 'Top that!'

The second guy calls the same girl over, pulls out $50, licks it and sticks it to her right cheek. Now they are both looking at the third guy, and he sees he has to do better than that. He thinks for a moment, calls the same girl over, gets out his credit card, swipes it down the crack, takes the $60 and heads for the door!

CRIMINALS

'You ever kept a diary, Bill?' asked prisoner Jim
'What's a diary?, replies his cellmate.
'A record of what a bloke does.'
'Nah, the police and gaolers do it for me.'

CROC

I'll have a crocodile sandwich with lettuce and tomato, mate — and make it snappy!

CUNTS

What do you call a jar full of cunts?
Clitorous all sorts.

What is the difference between a women's athletics team and tribe of pygmies?
The pygmies are a bunch of cunning runts.

CUSTOMER SERVICE

Boss: 'Our two goals this year are to downsize and to improve customer service.'
Wayne: 'How can you improve service if you're getting rid of service people?'
Boss: 'Who do you think is screwing up the customer service?'

D

DAD 'N' DAVE

Dave pulled the car over to the side of the road to show Dad where he'd first had sex. 'It was right down there by that tree. I remember the day plainly. It was a warm summer day. She and I were so much in love. We walked down to the tree and made love for hours,' said Dave.

'That sounds wonderful, son,' said Dad.

'Yes. It was OK until I looked up and noticed her mother was standing right there watching us.'

'Oh, my God! What did her mother say when she saw you making love to her daughter?'

'Baaaaaaa.'

Dad 'n' Dave go to town and, walking past a brothel, Dave says, 'Dad, I've never been to brothel. Can we go in?'

'Well son, so long as you don't tell your Mother.'

'OK, Dad.'

They each get a girl and go upstairs to adjoining rooms. As they go in Dad says to Dave. 'I bet I can fuck mine more times than you tonight, Dave!'

'Bet you a fiver I can do it more times than you, Dad, and to prove it, each time we have one, chalk it up on the wall.'

'OK.'

They go inside and before long there's moaning and groaning and goes on for hours. Finally Dave is stuffed. He looks at the wall to check; he has made three chalk marks on the wall.

'Ah, bet the old bugger can't beat three roots in a night.'

A knock on Dave's door. It is Dad. He comes into the room and sees the three chalk marks. 'Oh bugger it, Dave, 111 roots — you beat me by three!'

DAUGHTERS

A small town farmer had three daughters. Being a single father, he tended to be a little over-protective of his daughters. When men came to take his daughters out on a date, he would greet them with a shotgun to make sure they knew who was boss.

One evening, all his daughters were going out on dates. The doorbell rang, the farmer got his shotgun, and answered the door. A young man said, 'Hi, I'm Joe, I'm here for Flo, We're goin' to the show, Is she ready to go?' The farmer frowned but decided to let them go.

The doorbell rang again, the farmer got his shotgun, and answered the door. A young man said, 'Hi, I'm Eddie, I'm here for Betty, We gettin' spaghetti, Is she ready?' The farmer frowned but decided to let them go.

The doorbell rang again, the farmer got his shotgun, and answered the door. A gentlemen said, 'Hi, I'm Chuck.' And the farmer shot him.

DAYLIGHT SAVING

Why is South Australia half an hour behind the east coast?
To allow their brains time to catch up.

Why is there no daylight saving in Queensland?
Because Premier Jo thought there was enough sun shining out his arse.

Tasmanian daylight saving?
Um, what's daylight saving? How do you save it?

Victorian daylight saving?
Bewdie, more time for cricket and football.

DEATH

'It's funny how people love the dead.
Once you are dead you are made for life.'
　　　　　　　— Jimi Hendrix, singer/guitarist

'Death should not be seen as an end,
but as an efficient way to cut down on expenses.'
　　　　— Woody Allen, American actor/director

Why do men usually die before women?
They want to.

DEATHBED WORDS

I die hard but am not afraid to go.
— George Washington, US President, d.1799

I never felt better.
— Douglas Fairbanks Snr, Actor, d.1939

That was the best icecream soda I ever tasted.
— Lou Costello, comedian, d.1959

It is very beautiful over there.
— Thomas Edison, inventor, d.1931

I have offended God and mankind because my work did not reach the quality it should have.
— Leonardo da Vinci, artist, d.1519

I'm bored with it all.
— Winston Churchill, British prime minister, d.1957, just before he went into a coma. He died seven days later.

Either that wallpaper goes, or I do.
— Oscar Wilde, wit, d.1900

I should never have switched from Scotch to Martinis.
— Humphrey Bogart, actor, d.1957

I had a hell of a lot of fun and I've enjoyed every minute of it.
— Errol Flynn, Australian actor, d.1959

Go away, I'm all right.
> — H. G. Wells, novelist, d.1946

Such is life.
> — Edward 'Ned' Kelly, bushranger, folk hero, d.1880

Shoot straight you bastards and don't make as mess of it.
> — Harry 'Breaker' Morant, Australian poet and folk hero, shot by the British during the Boer War.

DEATH ROW

A chemist, a biologist and an electrical engineer were on death row waiting to go in the electric chair. The chemist was brought forward first.

'Do you have anything you want to say?' asked the executioner, strapping him in.

'No,' replied the chemist. The executioner flicked the switch and nothing happened. Under state law, if an execution attempt fails, the prisoner is released, so the chemist was released.

The biologist was brought forward. 'Do you have anything you want to say?'

'No, just get on with it.' The executioner flicked the switch, and again nothing happened, so the biologist was released.

Then the electrical engineer was brought forward. 'Do you have anything you want to say?' asked the executioner.

'Yes,' replied the engineer, 'If you swap the red and the blue wires over, you might make this thing work.'

DENTURES

A lady walks into the dentist's office, takes off her underwear, sits down on the chair and spreads her legs wide open.

'You must have made a mistake,' says the shocked dentist, 'The gynaecologist's office is one level higher.'

To that the lady replies, 'No mistake, you installed

my husband's dentures last week, now you'll be the one getting them out.'

DESERT ISLAND

An Aussie was marooned on a desert island. His only companions were a male dog and a female koala. The dog and koala hit it off, and for a year the Aussie could only sit and watch while the dog humped the koala senseless.

'Lucky Bastards!' thought the Aussie, 'I could do with a good shag myself'

One day a beautiful naked blonde was washed up on the beach. 'Hi. I'll do anything you want me to,' she said to the Aussie.

'Great! At last, after all this time! Take the dog for a walk, love, while I shag this koala!'

A man and his wife had been stranded on a deserted island for many years. The morning following a bad storm, a new guy washes up on the shore. The new guy and the wife are VERY attracted to each other right away, but they realise that certain protocols will have to be observed. The husband, oblivious to the pheromones floating around, is just glad to have someone new to talk to. 'This is wonderful! Now we'll be able to have three people doing 8-hour shifts in the watchtower instead of two people doing 12-hour shifts.' The new man is only too happy to help, and in fact volunteers to do the first shift. He climbs up the tall tower to stand watch, scanning the horizon for any ships.

Soon the husband and wife start placing stones in a circle in order to make a fire to cook supper. The new man yells down: 'Hey, no screwing!'

They look at each other and yell back: 'We're not screwing!'

A few minutes later, they start to put driftwood into the stone circle.

Again the new man yells down: 'Heeey, no screwing!'

Again they yell back, 'We're not screwing!'

Later they are putting palm leaves on the roof of the shack to patch leaks. Once again the new man yells down from high above: 'Hey, I said no screwing!!'

They yell back, 'And we said we're not screwing!'

At last the shift is over and the new man climbs down from the tower and the husband starts to climb up. By the time he gets halfway up, his wife and the new man are already screwing their brains out. Once at the top, the husband turns around and looks down and says to himself: 'Gees. From up here it DOES look like they're screwing.'

DID YOU HEAR?

Did you hear about the bloke who figured women out?
He died laughing before he could tell anyone.

DILDOES

Innocent young lady goes into a Brisbane Adult Shop. Very sheepishly she's asks the salesman.

'Um, do you have ... um, you know ... um ... sex aids?'

The salesman never bats an eyelid, 'You mean dildoes? Yeah sure.' He pulls out a box, puts it on the counter and starts to unloads them. 'We've got big ones, little ones, blue ones, black ones with ribs ...'

The embarrassed woman looks around shyly.

'Look, lady, you have a look through here while I go and serve those other customers,' and he walks off to the back of the shop. He returns a few minutes later, and the young lady has a big smile on her face.

'Chosen one, have we then?' he asks.

'Yes, thank you. I'll have this tartan one with the white knob on the top.'

'Sorry but you can't buy that one.'

'Why not'? she says disappointed.

'That's my thermos flask.'

A little old, blue-haired lady walks shakily into a porno shop. She can barely get to the counter because she's so wobbly. But she finally makes it, and asks the salesman in a shaky voice, 'Do you have di-ildoes?'

The clerk replies, 'Why, yes we do.'

The little old lady then asks, 'Do yo-u ha-ve one about si-ix inches long a-nd about two in-ches thick?'

The clerk politely replies, 'Yes, ma'am.'

'Does it ru-n on 2AA batter-ies?' she shakily asks. He nods, 'Yes.'

'Do y-ou know h-o——w to tu-rn the damn thi——ng o——ff?'

DISHWASHER

What do you do when the dishwasher won't work? Smack her arse.

DIVORCE PROCEEDINGS

A judge was interviewing a woman about her pending divorce, and asked, 'What are the grounds for your divorce?'

She replied, 'About four acres and a nice little home in the middle of the property with a stream running by.'

'No,' he said, 'I mean what is the foundation of this case?'

'It is made of concrete, brick and mortar,' she responded.

'I mean,' he continued, 'What are your relations like?'

'I have an aunt and uncle living here in town, and so do my husband's parents.'

He said, 'Do you have a real grudge?'

'No,' she replied, 'We have a two-car carport and have never really needed one.'

'Please,' he tried again, 'Is there any infidelity in your marriage?'

'Yes, both my son and daughter have stereo sets. We don't necessarily like the music, but the answer to your questions is yes.'

'Ma'am, does your husband ever beat you up?'

'Yes,' she responded, 'about twice a week he gets up earlier than I do.'

Finally, in frustration, the judge asked, 'Lady, why do you want a divorce?'

'Oh, I don't want a divorce,' she replied. 'I've never wanted a divorce. My husband does. He said he can't communicate with me.'

❓

If you are having sex with two women and another walks in what do you have?
Divorce proceedings probably.

DOCTORS

A woman accompanied her husband to the doctor's office for a checkup. Afterwards, the doctor took the wife aside and said, 'Unless you do the following things, your husband will surely die.' The doctor went on to say, 'Here's what you need to do. Every morning make sure you serve him a good healthy breakfast. Meet him at home each day for lunch so you can serve him a well balanced meal. Make sure you feed him a good, hot meal each evening and don't overburden him with any stressful conversation, nor ask him to perform any household chores. Also, keep the house spotless and clean so he doesn't get exposed to any threatening germs.'

On the way home, the husband asked his wife what the doctor said.

She replied, 'You're going to die.'

A man goes to his doctor and says, 'I don't think my wife's hearing is as good as it used to be, what should I do?'

The doctor replies, 'Try this test to find out for sure. When your wife is in the kitchen doing the dishes, stand five metres behind her and ask her a question, if she doesn't respond keep moving closer asking the question until she hears you.'

The man goes home and sees his wife preparing dinner. He stands five metres behind her and says, 'What's for dinner, dear?' No response.

He moves to three metres behind her and asks again. Again no response.

Two metres and still no answer.

Finally he stands directly behind her and says, 'Dear, what's for supper?'

She says, 'For the fourth time, I SAID CHICKEN!'

The man told his doctor that he wasn't able to do all the things around the house that he used to do. When the examination was complete, he said, 'Now, Doc, I can take it. Tell me in plain English what is wrong with me.'

'Well, in plain English,' the doctor replied, 'You're just lazy.'

'OK,' said the man. 'Now give me the medical term so I can tell my wife.'

An artist asked the gallery owner if there had been any interest in his paintings on display at that time.

'I have good news and bad news,' the owner replied. 'The good news is that a man asked about your work and wondered if it would appreciate in value after your death. When I told him it would, he bought all fifteen of your paintings.'

'That's wonderful!' the artist exclaimed. 'What's the bad news?'

'The guy was your doctor.'

A woman went to her doctor for advice. She told him that her husband had developed a penchant for anal sex, and she was not sure that it was such a good idea.

The doctor asked, 'Do you enjoy it?'

She said that she did.

He asked, 'Does it hurt you?'

She said that it didn't.

The doctor then told her, 'Well, then, there's no reason that you shouldn't practise anal sex, if that's what you like, so long as you take care not to get pregnant.'

The woman was mystified. She asked 'You can get pregnant from anal sex?'

The doctor replied, 'Of course. Where do you think lawyers come from?'

DOCTOR OF PSYCHOLOGY

A doctor of psychology was doing his morning rounds when he entered a patient's room. He found patient number one sitting on the floor, pretending to saw a piece of wood in half. Patient number two was hanging from the ceiling by his feet.

The doctor asked patient number one what he was doing. The patient replied, 'Can't you see I'm sawing this piece of wood in half?'

The doctor asked patient number one what number two was doing. Patient number one replied,

'Oh. He's my friend, but he's a little crazy. He thinks he's a light bulb.'

The doctor looks up and. notices patient number two's face is going all red, so he asks patient number one, 'If he's your friend, you should get him down from there before he hurts himself.'

Patient number one replies, 'What? And work in the dark?'

DOGS

A drunk staggers into the kitchen, where his annoyed wife sits at the table.

'You drunken sod, late again. I've given your tea to the dog.'

'You heartless woman,' bemoans the drunk. 'Now I'll have to buy a new dog.'

DOGS and CATS

A boy came home one day and asked his mum, 'What is a bitch and a pussy.'

Mum says, 'Well, a bitch is a female dog and a pussy is a cat.' The boy thinks to himself that that doesn't sound right since the other kids were calling each other that, so he goes to his dad and asks, 'What is a bitch and a pussy?' So Dad pulls out his *Playboy* and opens it to the centrefold. He draws a circle around the woman's pussy and says, 'Now that's a pussy, son! And everything else is the bitch!'

DOGS ARE BETTER THAN WOMEN

- Dogs don't cry.
- Dogs love it when your friends come over.
- Dogs don't care if you use their shampoo.
- Dogs think you sing well.
- Dogs don't expect you to call when you're running late.
- The later you are, the more excited dogs are to see you.
- Dogs will forgive you for playing with other dogs.
- Dogs don't notice if you call them by another dog's name.
- Dogs are excited by rough play.
- Dogs don't mind if you give their offspring away.
- Dogs love red meat.
- Dogs appreciate excessive body hair.
- Anyone can get a good-looking dog.

- If a dog is gorgeous, other dogs don't hate it.
- Dogs don't shop.
- Dogs like it when you leave lots of things on the floor.
- A dog's mood stays the same all month long.
- Dogs never need to examine the relationship.
- A dog's parents never visit.
- Dogs love long car trips.
- Dogs understand that instincts are better than asking for directions.
- Dogs understand that all animals smaller than dogs were made to be hunted.

- When a dog gets old and starts to snap at you endlessly, you can shoot it.
- Dogs like beer.
- Dogs don't hate their bodies.
- No dog ever bought a Mariah Carey album.
- No dog ever put on 50 kilos after reaching adulthood.
- Dogs never criticise.
- Dogs agree that you never have to raise your voice to get your point across.
- You never have to wait for a dog.
- Dogs have no use for flowers, cards or jewelry.
- Dogs don't borrow your shirts.
- Dogs never want foot-rubs.
- Dogs enjoy heavy petting in public.
- Dogs never expect gifts.
- It is legal to keep a dog chained up at your house.

- Dogs understand that farts are funny.
- Dogs don't worry about germs.
- Dogs don't want to know about every other dog you've ever had.
- Dogs like to do their snooping outside as opposed to in your wallet/desk or the back of your sock drawer.
- Dogs don't let magazine articles guide their lives.
- Dogs find you amusing when you are drunk.
- Dogs can't talk.
- Dogs aren't catty.
- Dogs seldom outlive you.

WHAT DO DOGS AND WOMEN HAVE IN COMMON?

Both look stupid in hats.
Both can eat two kilos of chocolate in one sitting.
Neither understand football.
Both look good in fur.

Both are good at pretending they are listening to every word you say.
Neither believe that silence is golden.
Both constantly want back-rubs.
Neither has any understanding of money.
You can never tell what they are thinking.

DONATIONS

The staff at a local charity office realised that it had never received a donation from the town's most successful lawyer. The person in charge of contributions called him to persuade him to contribute and said, 'Our research shows that out of a yearly income of at least $500,000, you give not a penny to charity. Wouldn't you like to give back to the community in some way?'

The lawyer mulled this over for a moment and replied, 'Firstly, did your research also show that my mother is dying after a long illness and has medical bills that are several times her annual income?'

Embarrassed, the charity worker mumbled, 'Um … No.'

'Or,' the lawyer continued, 'that my brother, a disabled veteran, is blind and confined to a wheelchair?'

The stricken charity worker began to stammer out an apology but was interrupted when the lawyer added, 'Or that my sister's husband died in a traffic accident,' the lawyer's voice rising in indignation, 'leaving her penniless with three children?'

Humiliated the charity worker, completely beaten, said simply, 'I had no idea …'

On a roll, the lawyer cut him off once again, 'So if I don't give any money to them, why should I give any to you?'

DOOMED

Sometimes, it seems as if some people are just plain 'fated'. If you don't believe it, consider these weird stories:

A fierce gust of wind blew 45-year-old Vittorio's car into a river in 1983. He managed to break a window, climb out and swim to shore — where a tree blew over and killed him.

Mike, 31, was filming a movie in 1983 on the dangers of low-level bridges when the truck he was standing on passed under a low-level bridge — killing him.

Walter, a 26-year-old salesman, was so afraid of dentists that in 1979 he asked a fellow worker to try to cure his toothache by punching him in the jaw. The punch caused Walter to fall down, hitting his head, and he died of a fractured skull.

George, owner of a factory, narrowly escaped death when a 1983 blast flattened his factory except for one wall. After treatment for minor injuries, he returned to the scene to search for files. The remaining wall then collapsed on him, killing him.

In 1981, depressed since he could not find a job, 42-year-old Romolo sat in his kitchen with a gun in his hand threatening to kill himself. His wife pleaded for him not to do it, and after about an hour he burst into tears and threw the gun to the floor. It went off and killed his wife.

In 1983 Mrs Carson was laid out in her coffin, presumed dead of heart disease. As mourners watched, she suddenly sat up. Her daughter dropped dead of fright; killed by a heart attack.

A man hit by a car in 1977 got up uninjured, but lay back down in front of the car when a bystander told him to pretend he was hurt so he could collect the insurance money. The car rolled forward and crushed him to death.

Surprised while burgling a house a thief fled out through the back door, clambered over a nine-foot wall, dropped down and found himself in the city prison.

In 1976 22-year-old Bob was crossing a busy road when he was struck by a taxi and flung over its roof. The taxi drove away and, as Bob lay stunned in the road, another car ran into him, rolling him into the gutter. It too drove on. As a knot of gawkers gathered, a delivery van ploughed through the crowd, leaving in its wake three injured bystanders and an even more battered Bob. When a fourth vehicle came along, the crowd wisely scattered and only one person was hit — Bob. In the space of two minutes he suffered a fractured skull, broken pelvis, broken leg, and other assorted injuries. Hospital officials said he would recover.

While motorcycling through the countryside, Chris came up to a railway line just as the crossing gates were coming down. While he sat idling, he was joined by a farmer with a goat, which the farmer tethered to the crossing gate. A few moments later a horse and cart drew up behind Chris, followed in short order by a man in a sports car. When the train roared through the crossing, the horse startled and bit Chris on the arm. Not a man to be trifled with, Chris responded by punching the horse in the head. As a result the horse's owner jumped down from his cart and began scuffling with the motorcyclist. The horse, not up to this sort of excitement, backed away briskly, smashing the cart into the sports car. At this, the sports-car driver leapt out of his car and joined the fray. The farmer came forward to try to pacify the three flailing men. As he did so, the crossing gates rose and his goat was strangled. At last report, the insurance companies were still trying to sort out the claims.

Two motorists had an all-too-literal head-on collision in heavy fog. Each was guiding his car at a snail's pace near the centre of the road. At the moment of impact their heads were both out of the windows when they smacked together. Both men were hospitalised with severe head injuries. Their cars weren't scratched.

DRINKERS

One day two Aussies walked into a pub together. A Pommie was seated at the bar. They each proceeded to buy a large beer. Just as they were about to enjoy their creamy beverage, a fly landed in each of their glasses and became stuck in the thick head. The two Aussies pushed their beers away in disgust. The Pommie fished the offending fly out and held it over the beer and yelled, 'SPIT IT OUT! SPIT IT OUT, YOU BASTARD!'

DUCK HUNTER

A man wakes up early one morning and decides to go duck hunting. He tells his wife, 'You've got three choices; you can go duck hunting with me, I'll do ya anally or you can give me a blowjob. I'm gonna load up the ute and get the dog out. Make up your mind before I get back.'

Hubby returns twenty minutes later and says, 'Well, what's it going to be?'

She says, 'There's no way I'm going duck hunting and you're not doing me up the arse, so I guess it's a blowjob.'

A couple of minutes later she starts choking and spitting and says, 'Jesus, you taste like shit.'

'Oh yeah,' he replies, 'The dog didn't want to go duck huntin' either.'

DUNNY

What is the difference between a woman and a dunny?
A dunny doesn't follow you around.

ELEPHANTS!

What did Tarzan say when he saw the elephants coming over the hill?
'Here come the elephants over the hill.'

What did Tarzan say when he saw the elephants coming over the hill wearing dark sunglasses?
Nothing, he didn't recognise them.

Why do elephants wear pink tennis shoes?
Because white ones get dirty too fast.

Why do elephants have wrinkled ankles?
Because their tennis shoes are too tight.

Why do elephants have wrinkled knees?
From playing marbles.

How do you tell an elephant from a grape?
A grape is purple.

What did Jane say when she saw the elephants?
'OOH, look at all those grapes.' (She was colour blind.)

Why are elephants coloured grey?
So you can tell them from canaries.

What is it that looks like an elephant and flies and is very dangerous?
A flying elephant with a machine gun.

Why do elephants float down the river on their backs?
So they won't get their tennis shoes wet.

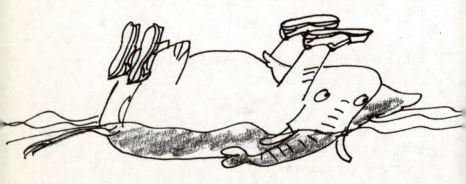

If you're colour blind, how do you tell an elephant from a grape?
Jump around on it for a while. If you don't get any wine, it's an elephant.

What is it that looks like an elephant and flies?
A flying elephant.

Why don't more elephants go to college?
Not too many elephants finish high school.

How do you put six elephants in a Volkswagen?
Three in the front and three in the back.

Why do elephants need trunks?
Because they don't have glove compartments.

How do you know if an elephant's standing near you in a lift?
By the smell of peanuts on his breath.

Why do elephants prefer peanuts to caviar?
Because they're easier to get at the movies.

Why do elephants have flat feet?
From jumping out of trees.

What do you call elephants who ride on trains?
Passengers.

Why do girl elephants wear angora sweaters?
So you can tell them from boy elephants.

Why don't elephants use bathtubs?
They do use bathtubs — for beach hats.

Why don't elephants like blue lace petticoats?
Who said they don't like blue lace petticoats?

Where do baby elephants come from?
BIG storks.

Why do elephants lie on their backs with their feet in the air?
So they can trip birds.

Why do elephants have hair on their tails?
Why not?

How does an elephant put his trunk in a crocodile's mouth?
VERY carefully.

How can you tell if an elephant is sleeping?
When he's in bed with the covers pulled up and he's wearing pajamas and his pink tennis shoes are off, the chances are he's asleep, if he's snoring. But watch it anyway.

Why did the elephants quit their job at the factory?
They got tired of working for peanuts.

Why do elephants eat peanuts?
Because they're saltier than prunes.

Where do you find elephants?
It depends where you lost them.

How do you make a hamburger for an elephant?
First, you take 500 jars of mustard, 100 litres of tomato sauce, 50 kilos of onions, and then you get this BIG roll ...

What did the elephant say when the Volkswagen ran into it?
'How many times have I told you kids — don't play in the street!'

What do elephants eat beside hamburgers?
Canned elephant food.

What did General de Gaulle say when he saw the elephants coming over the hill?
'Voilà, les éléphants over the hill.'

What did the elephants say to General de Gaulle?
Nothing, elephants don't speak French.

Why don't elephants take trains during rush hour?
They're afraid of pickpockets.

What does an elephant smell like before it takes a shower?
An elephant.

Why did the elephant walk around in polka-dot socks?
Somebody stole his tennis shoes.

What does an elephant smell like after it takes a shower?
A wet elephant.

Why don't elephants like martinis?
Did you ever try to get an olive out of your nose?

What do you do when an elephant sneezes?
Get out of the way.

How do elephants see at night?
Not very well — unless they take off their dark glasses.

Why aren't more elephants called Walter?
Because Ed and Norm are better names for elephants.

What do you do when an elephant sneezes?
Get out of the way.

How does an elephant get into a phone booth?
The same way he got out.

What did the nearsighted elephant say when he saw the tank?
'Hi, Dad.'

What did Jane say when she saw the elephant working in the shoeshop?
'I didn't know the giraffe sold the place.'

What did Tarzan say when he saw the male elephant jump off the cliff?
'That's how the bull bounces.'

How can you tell when an elephant is getting ready to charge?
He takes out his Mastercard.

How do you housebreak an elephant?
You get fourteen copies of the *Sydney Morning Herald* — the Saturday edition.

What did the elephant say when he got caught in the revolving door?
'If this place wants to do much business with elephants, they better get bigger revolving doors!'

What's another name for an elephant beside Ed, Norm and Walter?
Lucille.

How do elephants keep their hides so shiny?
They use that greasy elephant stuff.

What do you call a hippopotamus who's been carrying elephants across the river all day?
A VERY tired hippopotamus.

Why do elephants squirt water through their noses?
If they squirted it through their tails, it'd be very difficult to aim.

What does a bald elephant wear for a toupée?
A sheep.

What did the banana say to the elephant?
Nothing, bananas can't talk.

Why do the elephants make fun of Tarzan?
They think his nose is funny.

Why don't elephants watch re-runs on television?
They didn't like the show the first time.

Why don't elephants named Ed eat meat on Fridays?
They're vegetarians.

What did the elephant say to the maharajah?
'Get off my back.'

Why does an elephant never forget?
What's he got to remember? Does an elephant have to remember where he parked his car, or his wedding anniversary, or whether he left the tap running in the kitchen?

Why do elephants jump across rivers?
So they won't step on the fish.

EMBARRASSED

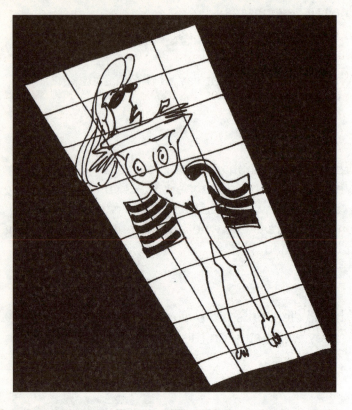

Joan, a rather well-proportioned though near-sighted secretary, spent almost all of her holiday sunbathing on the roof of her hotel in Perth. She wore a bathing suit the first few days, but always removed her glasses for an even face tan.

After several days she decided that no one could see her way up there, so she slipped out of her suit for an overall tan. She'd hardly begun when she heard someone running up the stairs; she was lying on her stomach, so she just pulled a towel over her bottom.

'Excuse me, miss,' said the flustered assistant manager of the hotel, out of breath from running up the stairs. 'The hotel doesn't mind your sunbathing on the roof, but we would very much appreciate your wearing a bathing suit as you have for the past week.'

'What difference does it make?' Joan asked rather calmly. 'No one can see me up here, and besides, I'm covered with a towel.'

'Not exactly,' said the embarrassed man. 'You're lying on the dining-room skylight!'

ENGINEERS

What is the difference between mechanical engineers and civil engineers?
Mechanical engineers build weapons. Civil engineers build targets.

The graduate with an engineering degree asks, 'How does it work?'
'The graduate with a science degree asks, 'Why does it work?'
The graduate with an accounting degree asks, 'How much will it cost?'
The graduate with an arts degree asks, 'Do you want fries with that?'

The optimist says, 'The glass is half full.'
The pessimist says, 'The glass is half empty.'
The engineer says, 'Who made the fucking glass twice as big as it needs to be.'

ERECTION

This guy has a crush on a girl at his work. He is dying to ask her out on a date, but every time he sees her he gets the biggest erection ever. There is nothing he can do to control it. After some time, he decides to get her phone number and call her up. This way he won't have to see her and he won't get too excited. He ends up asking her out and she says yes. He decides to tie his penis to his leg so when he sees her she'll never notice it. He gets to her house. When he knocks on her door, she answers the door wearing a sheer teddy. He kicks her in the face.

ESKIMO

What is a Ig?
An eskimo's house without a loo.

FAITH

A man is in his house when horrendous rains come up. The water starts rising, and before you know it, we're talking major flood. Roads are covered. Nothing's moving.

Pretty soon, a boat comes along. The man in the boat yells, 'Come on — we're here to save you. Get into the boat.'

The man in the house says, 'No, I've got faith that God will save me.'

The boat leaves. The water keeps rising. The man is forced up the second floor of his house by the flood waters. Another boat comes along. The man in the boat yells, 'Come on! It's getting worse. If you don't get into the boat, you're going to drown.'

From the second-floor window the guy says, 'No, I'll be OK. I've got faith in God that he'll save me.'

The boat leaves. Water's rising. The man's on the roof. A helicopter hovers overhead and the pilot shouts out, 'This is your last chance. Climb up the ladder. If you don't come now you're going to drown.'

The guy says from the roof, 'No, thanks. God will save me.'

The pilot shrugs his shoulders and leaves. The water rises. The guy drowns. He ascends to the pearly gates. He asks St Peter, 'What happened? I've been devoted to God and had absolute faith that he would save me. Why did he let me down?'

And St Peter asks him, 'What more do you want? God sent you two boats and a helicopter!'

FALLING FOR WOMEN

Two Kiwis are working on a building site in Auckland. Phul (Phil) and Muck (Mick). Phul turns to Muck and says, 'Cawww, I've gotta take a puss, but there's nowhere to go, eh?'

'Walk out to the ind of thit plank,' replies Muck.

'I'll stand on this ind and balance ut.'

So out goes Phul to take a piss. The lunch siren sounds, Muck forgets what he's supposed to be doing, steps off the plank and Phul is a goner.

Several months later an Australian, a Frenchman and a bloke from NZ are sitting in a bar discussing which of their respective nations chase women the hardest ...

Wazza the Aussie says, 'Mate, I've been known to miss a piss-up session down the pub with me mates because I've been trying to crack on to sheilas!'

Pierre, the Frenchman, says, 'No, no, no, ve French chase ze women with much zest and give them gifts to win zem over!'

Meanwhile Bob, the Kiwi, sits laughing and says, 'Now, you blokes are both wrong. The other day I was walking past a building site in Auckland following these two gorgeous-looking birds, and this bloke comes plummeting from the sky with his dick in his hand screaming, 'FUUUUUUUUUCKKKK MEEEEEEE!'

FAMOUS QUOTES

According to a new survey, women say they feel more comfortable undressing in front of men than they do undressing in front of other women. They say that women are too judgemental, where, of course, men are just grateful.

— Jay Leno

Men look at women the way men look at cars. Everyone looks at Ferraris. Now and then we like a pick-up truck, and we all buy stationwagons.

— Tim Allen

There's very little advice in men's magazines, because men don't think there's a lot they don't know. Women do. Women want to learn. Men think, 'I know what I'm doing, just show me somebody naked.'

— Jerry Seinfeld

I am a marvellous housekeeper. Every time I leave a man I keep his house.

— Zsa Zsa Gabor

FARTS

In a Manly home for the aged there's an old bloke being visited by his daughter. The old man is very happy to see his daughter. She asks him, 'How's everything?'

He leans over in his wheelchair and the nurses immediately push him back. He leans over in his wheelchair again and the nurses push him back up.

'The problem here is they won't let you have a good fart!' he replies.

Why do men fart more than women?
Because women won't shut up long enough for the pressure to build up.

FEMALE TO FEMALE

Two women were fixing their make-up in a restaurant toilet mirror.

'Helen, I can't help but notice, you are wearing your wedding ring on the wrong finger of the wrong hand.'

'Because,' replied the other woman, 'I married the wrong man!'

FIGHTER

'I nearly got into a fight because of you the other night, Burkie,' said Pat.

'Why, what do you mean?' asked a puzzled Burkie.

'Well, some smart bastard down the end of the bar yelled out loud that that Burke bastard wasn't fit to live with the pigs. But, I really stuck up for you, mate. I told them you were!'

FIRE ALARM

Husband and wife were going to a costume party. The husband didn't know what to wear. His wife told him to hurry or they would be late for the party. She walked out of the bedroom completely naked, except for a big old floppy pair of boots on her feet.

'Where's your costume?' the husband asked.

'This is it,' replied his wife.

'What sort of costume is that?' asked the husband.

'Why, I am going as Puss-in-Boots,' explains the wife. 'Now hurry and get your costume on.'

The husband went upstairs and was back in about two minutes. He too was completely naked, except for a rose vase slid over his penis.

'What kind of costume is that?' asked the wife.

'I am a fire alarm,' he replied.

'A fire alarm?' she repeated laughing.

'Yes,' he replied. 'In case of fire break the glass, pull twice and I come.'

FIREMEN

Why do firemen have bigger balls than policemen? They sell more tickets.

FIRST AID

A woman rushed to the fallen man. He was surrounded by his mates and was clutching his hands over his groin. She explained that she was a physical therapist and that she could relieve his pain if he'd allow her to do it. After some convincing, he finally agreed. She gently took his hands away. She loosened his pants, and she put her hands inside. She began to massage him.

'How does that feel?' she asked after a while noticing his smile.

'It feels great thanks, love, but my thumb still hurts like hell.'

FISHING

A couple went on vacation to a fishing resort near a national park. The husband liked to fish at the crack of dawn; the wife preferred to read.

One morning the husband returned after several hours of fishing and decided to take a short nap. The wife thought she'd take the boat out. She was not familiar with the lake. She rowed out, anchored the boat, and started reading her book.

Along comes the park ranger in his boat, pulls up alongside and says, 'Good morning, Missus. What are you doing?'

'Reading my book,' she replies as she thinks to herself, 'Is this guy blind, or what?'

'You're in a no-fishing area,' he informs her.

'But, officer, I'm not fishing. Can't you see that?'

'But you have all this equipment. I'll have to take you in and charge you.'

'If you do that I will charge you with rape,' snaps the irate woman.

'I didn't even touch you,' grouses the ranger.

'Yes, that's true, but you have all the equipment.'

FIVE DOCTORS

Five surgeons were taking a tea break and were discussing their work. The first said, 'I think accountants are the easiest to operate on. You open them up and everything inside is numbered.'

The second said, 'I think librarians are the easiest to operate on. You open them up and everything inside is in alphabetical order.'

The third said, 'I like to operate on electricians. You open them up and everything inside is colour-coded.'

The fourth one said, 'I like to operate on lawyers. They're heartless, spineless, gutless, and their heads and their arses are interchangeable.'

The fifth surgeon said, 'I like engineers … they always understand when you have a few parts left over at the end …'

FIVE STAGES of BEING DRUNK

Stage 1 — SMART
This is when you suddenly become an expert on every subject in the known universe. You know you know everything and you want to pass on your knowledge to anyone who will listen. At this stage you are always RIGHT. And of course, the person you are talking to is very WRONG. This makes for an interesting argument when both parties are SMART.

Stage 2 — GOOD LOOKING
This is when you realise that you are the BEST-LOOKING person in the entire bar and that people fancy you. You can go up to a perfect stranger knowing they fancy you and really want to talk to you. Bear in mind that you are still SMART, so you can talk to this person about any subject under the sun.

Stage 3 — RICH
This is when you suddenly become the richest person in the world. You can buy drinks for the entire bar because you have an armoured truck full of money parked behind the bar. You can also make bets at this stage, because of course you're still SMART, so naturally, you will win all your bets. It

doesn't matter how much you bet because you are RICH. You will also buy drinks for everyone that you fancy, because you are now the BEST-LOOKING person in the world.

Stage 4 — BULLET PROOF

You are now ready to pick fights with anyone and everyone, especially those with whom you have been betting or arguing. This is because nothing can hurt you. At this point you can also go up to the partners of the people who you fancy and challenge them to a battle of the wits or money. You have no fear of losing this battle, because you are smart, you're RICH, and Hell — you're better looking than them anyway!

Stage 5 — INVISIBLE

This is the final stage of drunkenness. At this point you can do anything, because NO ONE CAN SEE YOU. You dance on a table to impress the people you fancy because the rest of the people in the room cannot see you. You can also snog the face off them because the rest of the people in the room cannot see you. You are also invisible to the person who wants to fight you. You can walk through the street singing at the top of your lungs because no one can see or hear you and because you're still SMART you know ALL the words.

Sound familiar?

FLAT-CHESTED

How do you really know when a woman is flat-chested?
She wears suspenders to hold up her bra.

How can a woman tell if she is flat-chested?
When she looks down the only bumps she sees are her kneecaps.

FLOSSIE and BESSIE

Flossie and Bessie are sitting on the front porch, rocking back and forth in their rocking chairs, on a hot Queensland summer evening.

They pass the time talking about anything and everything:

Flossie: 'Bessie, have I told you about my lovers?'
Bessie: 'Lovers? What do you mean lovers?'
Flossie: 'My three lovers that I've been seeing.'
Bessie (shocked): 'Well, I'll be! How on earth do you keep from getting them mixed up?'
Flossie (proudly): 'Well, I have named them all after soft drinks.'
Bessie: 'Soft drinks? What on earth do you mean?'
Flossie: 'The first I call 7-up. 'Cause he's got seven inches and he is always up!'
Bessie (snickers and blushes).
Flossie: 'My second I call Mountain Dew. 'Cause I'm just a mountain and he will always do!'
Bessie (blushes, more and more snickering).
Flossie: 'And my third I call Jack Daniels.'
Bessie (interrupting): 'Jack Daniels? That's not a soft drink! That's a hard liquor!'
Flossie: 'EXACTLY!'

FOOD WAITER

François, the arrogant French waiter, works for a well-known Sydney restaurant. Brian and Barbara are enjoying their eighth wedding anniversary and look forward to the joy of a quiet and lovely dinner.

As François carries their meals towards them, Barbara is horrified and nods to Brian. 'Hey mate, you've got your thumbs stuck in our steaks,' complains Brian. Without missing a beat the waiter thrusts the plates before them and turns to walk off, 'You don't want me to drop them again, do you?'

FOOTBALL

Three football fans were on their way to a game when one noticed a foot sticking out of the bushes by the side of the railway line. They stopped and discovered a nude woman, drunk and passed out.

Out of respect and propriety, the Essendon fan took off his cap and put it over her right breast. The Melbourne fan took of his cap and placed it over her left breast. Following their lead, the Collingwood fan took off his cap and placed it over her crotch.

The police were called and an officer arrived and conducted his inspection. First, he lifted up the Essendon cap, replaced it, and wrote down some notes. Next, he lifted the Melbourne cap, replaced it, and wrote down some more notes. Then he lifted

the Collingwood cap, replaced it, lifted it again, replaced it, lifted it a third time, and replaced it one last time.

The Collingwood fan was getting upset and finally asked 'What are you, a pervert or something? Why do you keep lifting and looking, lifting and looking?'

'Well,' said the officer, 'I'm simply surprised. Normally when I look under a Collingwood cap, I find an arsehole.'

FORD v. ADAM

Henry Ford dies and goes to Heaven. At the gates, St Peter tells Ford, 'Well, you've been such a good guy and your invention the car changed the world. As a reward, you can hang out with anyone you want.'

So Henry Ford thinks about it and says: 'I want to hang out with Adam, the first man.' St Peter at the gates points Adam out to Ford.

Ford goes over to Adam and asks, 'Hey, aren't you the inventor of woman?'

Adam says: 'Yes.'

'Well,' says Ford, 'You have some major design flaws in your invention:

1   There is too much front end protrusion;
2   It chatters at high speeds;
3   The rear end wobbles too much; and
4   The intake is too close to the exhaust.'

'Hmmmmm,' says Adam, 'Hold on.' Adam goes to the celestial computer, types in a few keystrokes, and waits for the results.

The computer prints out a slip of paper and Adam reads it.

He then says to Ford, 'It may be that my invention is flawed but, according to the stellar computer, more men are riding my invention than yours.'

FOREPLAY

What do you call pulling off a woman's pantyhose? Foreplay.

FORESKIN

A Jewish boy was walking with his girlfriend on the grounds of his father's house. His father was a successful doctor, and was carrying out a circumcision in the on-site surgery. As they were walking, they heard a scream. A foreskin flew out of the window and landed at the girl's feet.

'What's this,' she asked.

'Taste it,' he replied, 'If you like it, I'll give you a whole one!'

FROG AND THE PRINCESS

A huge muscular man walks into a bar and orders a beer. The bartender hands him the beer and says, 'You know, I'm not gay but I want to compliment you on your physique, it really is phenomenal! I have a question though, why is your head so small?'

The big guy nods slowly. He's obviously fielded this question many times. 'One day,' he begins, 'I was hunting when I got lost in the woods. I heard someone crying for help and finally realised that it was coming from a frog sitting on a rock next to me. "Kiss me. Kiss me and I will turn into a genie and grant you three wishes."

'So I looked around to make sure I was alone and gave the frog a kiss. POOF! The frog turned into a beautiful, voluptuous, naked woman. She said, "You now have three wishes."

'I looked down at my scrawny 70 kilo body and said, "I want a body like Arnold Schwarzeneger."

'She nodded, whispered a spell, and POOF! there I was, so huge that I ripped out of my clothes and was standing there naked!

'She then asked, "What will be your second

wish?" I looked hungrily at her beautiful body and replied, "I want to make sensuous love with you here by this stream." She nodded, lay down, and beckoned to me. We then made love for hours!

'Later, as we lay there next to each other, sweating from our glorious lovemaking, she whispered into my ear, "You know, you do have one more wish. What will it be?"

'I looked at her and replied, "How about a little head?"

Once upon a time, in a land far away, a beautiful, independent, self-assured princess happened upon a frog as she sat, contemplating ecological issues on the shores of an unpolluted pond in a verdant meadow near her castle.

A frog hopped into the princess's lap and said: 'Elegant Lady, I was once a handsome prince, until an evil witch cast a spell upon me. One kiss from you, however, and I will turn back into the dapper, young prince that I was and then, my sweet, we can marry and set up housekeeping in yon castle with my mother, where you can prepare my meals, clean my clothes, bear my children, and forever feel grateful and happy doing so.'

That night, as the princess dined sumptuously on a repast of lightly sautéed frog-legs seasoned in a white wine and onion cream sauce, she chuckled to herself and thought: 'I don't think so.'

FUCK

The most interesting and colourful word in the English language. It can be used as a verb, both transitive (John fucked Mary) and intransitive (Mary was fucked by John). It can be an action verb (John really gives a fuck), a passive verb (Mary really doesn't give a fuck), an adverb (Mary is fucking interested in John), or as a noun (Mary is a terrific fuck). It can also be used as an adjective (Mary is fucking beautiful) or an interjection (Fuck! I'm late for my date with Mary). It can even be used as a conjunction (Mary is easy, fuck, she's also stupid). As you can see, there are very few words with the overall versatility of the word 'fuck'.

Aside from its sexual connotations, this incredible word can be used to describe many situations:

Greetings: 'How the fuck are ya?'
Fraud: 'I got fucked by the car dealer.'

Resignation: 'Oh, fuck it!'
Trouble: 'I guess I'm fucked now.'
Aggression: 'FUCK YOU!'
Disgust: 'Fuck me.'
Confusion: 'What the fuck …?'
Difficulty: 'I don't understand this fucking business!'
Despair: 'Fucked again …'
Pleasure: 'I couldn't be fucking happier.'
Displeasure: 'What the fuck is going on here?'
Lost: 'Where the fuck are we?'
Disbelief: 'UNFUCKINGBELIEVABLE!'
Retaliation: 'Up your fucking arse!'
Denial: 'I didn't fucking do it.'
Perplexity: 'I know fuck about it.'
Apathy: 'Who really gives a fuck, anyhow?'
Suspicion: 'Who the fuck are you?'
Panic: 'Let's get the fuck out of here.'
Directions: 'Fuck off.'
Disbelief: 'How the fuck did you do that?'
Instruction: 'Get fucked!'
Suggestion: 'Go fuck yourself.'

It can be used in an anatomical description:'He's a fucking arsehole.'
It can be used to tell time: 'It's five fucking thirty.'
It can be used in business: 'How did I wind up with this fucking job?'
It can be maternal: 'Motherfucker.'
It can be political: 'Fuck John Howard!'

It has also been used throughout history:
'What the fuck was that?'

— Mayor of Hiroshima

'Where did all these fucking Indians come from?'
— General George A. Custer

'Where the fuck is all this water coming from?'
— Captain of the *Titanic*

'That's not a real fucking gun.'
— John Lennon

'Who's gonna fucking find out?'
— Richard Nixon

'Heads are going to fucking roll.'
— Anne Boleyn

'Who let the fucking woman drive?'
— Commander of Space Shuttle Challenger

'What fucking map?'
— Mark Thatcher

'Any fucking idiot could understand that.'
— Albert Einstein

'It does so fucking look like her!'
— Picasso

'How the fuck did you work that out?'
— Pythagoras

'Fuck a duck.'
— Walt Disney

'Why? Because it's fucking there!'
— Sir Edmund Hillary

'I don't suppose it's gonna fucking rain?'
— Joan of Arc

'Scattered fucking showers my arse.'
— Noah

'I need this parade like I need a fucking hole in my head.'
— John F. Kennedy

'Bow fucking Wow.'
— Scooby Doo

'You want what on the fucking ceiling?'
— Michelangelo

G

GENIE

A couple was golfing one day on a very exclusive golf course, lined with million-dollar houses. On the third tee the husband said, 'Dear, be very careful when you drive the ball — don't knock out any windows. It'll cost us a fortune to fix.' The wife teed up and shanked it right through the window of the biggest house on the course.

The husband cringed and said, 'I told you to watch out for the houses! All right, let's go up and apologise and see how much this is going to cost.'

They walked up, knocked on the door, and heard a voice say, 'Come on in.' They opened the door and saw glass all over the floor and a broken bottle lying on its side in the foyer. A man on the couch said, 'Are you the people who broke my window?'

'Uh, yeah. Sorry about that.' the husband replied.

'No, actually I want to thank you — I'm a genie who has been trapped for a thousand years in that bottle. You've released me. I'm allowed to grant three wishes — I'll give you each one wish, and I'll keep the last one for myself.'

'OK, great!' the husband said. 'I want a million dollars a year for the rest of my life.'

'No problem — it's the least I could do. And you, what do you want?' the genie said, looking at the wife.

'I want a house in every country of the world,' she said.

'Consider it done.' the genie replied.

'And what's your wish, genie?' the husband said.

'Well, since I've been trapped in that bottle, I haven't had sex with a woman in a thousand years. My wish is to sleep with your wife.'

The husband looked at the wife and said, 'Well, we did get a lot of money and all those houses. I suppose I don't mind.'

The genie took the wife upstairs and ravished her for two hours. After it was over, the genie rolled over, looked at the wife, and said, 'How old is your husband, anyway?'

'Thirty-five,' she replied.

'And he still believes in genies — that's amazing.'

A man was walking along the beach at Manly and stumbled across an old lamp. He picked it up, rubbed it and out popped a genie.

The genie said 'OK, OK. You released me from the lamp, blah, blah, blah. This is the fourth time this month and I'm getting a little sick of these wishes so you can forget about three. You only get one wish!'

The man sat and thought about it for a while and said, 'I've always wanted to go to Hawaii but I'm scared of flying and I get very seasick. Would you build me a bridge to Hawaii so I can drive there instead?'

The genie laughed and said, 'That's impossible. Think of the logistics of that! How would the supports ever reach the bottom of the Pacific? Think how much concrete ... how much steel ... ! No, have another wish.'

The man said OK and tried to think of a really good wish. Finally, he said, 'I've been married and divorced four times. My wives always said that I don't care and that I'm insensitive. So, I wish that I could understand women ... know how they feel inside and what they're thinking when they give me the silent treatment ... know why they are crying, know what they really want when they say "nothing" ... know how to make them truly happy ...'

The genie replied, 'You want that bridge two lanes or four?'

GEORGIE

Georgie porgie pudding and pie,
Jerked off in his girlfriend's eye,
When her eye was dry and shut,
Georgie fucked that one-eyed slut!

GETTING LAID

A young playboy took a blind date to an amusement park. They went for a ride on the Ferris wheel. The ride completed, she seemed rather bored. 'What would you like to do next?' he asked.

'I wanna get weighed,' she said. So the young man took her over to the weight guesser.

'Eighty-two kilos,' said the man at the scale, and he was absolutely right.

Next they rode the roller-coaster. After that, he bought her some popcorn and candyfloss, then he asked what else she would like to do.

'I wanna get weighed,' she said, seeming slightly annoyed. He had really latched onto a weird one tonight, thought the young man, and using the excuse he had developed a headache, he took the girl home.

The girl's mother was surprised to see her home so early, and asked, 'What's wrong, dear, didn't you have a nice time tonight?'

'Wousy,' said the girl.

GETTING THE JOB DONE

Whenever there was an important job to be done,
Everybody was sure that
Somebody would do it.
Anybody could have done it,

But Nobody did it.
When Nobody did it,
Everybody got angry
Because it was Everybody's job.
Everybody thought that
Somebody would do it,
But Nobody realised that
Nobody would do it.
So consequently Everybody blamed Somebody,
When Nobody did what Anybody
Could have done in the first place.

GOD

Why did god make men first?
He didn't want a woman looking over his shoulder while he worked.

God created all men equal ... only some of us a more fucking equal than others!

God isn't a woman, otherwise sperm would taste like chocolate.

GOLFERS

'Old golfers never die, they just lose their balls.'

TRAINING HINTS FOR GOLF
AND/OR TAKING A LEAK IN PUBLIC

1. Back straight, knees bent, feet shoulder width apart.
2. Form a loose grip.
3. Keep your head down.
4. Avoid a quick backswing.
5. Stay out of the water.
6. Try not to hit anyone.
7. If you are taking too long, please let others go ahead of you.
8. Don't stand directly in front of others.

9 Quiet please!... while others are preparing to go.
10 Don't take extra strokes.

The room was full of pregnant women and their partners. The Lamaze class was in full swing. The instructor was teaching the women how to breathe properly, and informing the men how to give the necessary assurances at this stage of the plan.

'Ladies, exercise is good for you,' announced the teacher. 'Walking is especially beneficial. And, gentlemen, it wouldn't hurt you to take the time to go walking with your partner!'

The room was very quiet. Finally, a man in the middle of the group raised his hand.

'Yes?' asked the instructor.

'Is it all right if she carries a golf bag while we walk?'

Two friends were getting ready to tee off on the first hole of a posh Queensland golf resort course. The first fellow steps up to the tee, places his ball, steps back to line up his shot, waggles his driver for several moments, then steps back to take several practice swings.

His partner tired of all this asked him why he was taking so long to make his drive.

To this the first player replies, 'My wife is at the club house watching and I want to get this shot just right.'

'Don't bother', his partner retorts. 'You'll never hit her from here.'

There was a man who was playing golf and put three golf balls in his pocket. When another man came up and asked him what was in his pocket the first guy said golf balls then the second guy asked is that like tennis elbow.

Can you tell the difference between a golf ball and a G-Spot?
A bloke will spend 20 minutes looking for a golf ball.

GOOD, BAD, WORSE

Good: You and your spouse agree, no more kids.
Bad: The birth control pills are missing.
Worse: Your daughter borrowed them.

Good: Your son studies a lot in his room.
Bad: You find several porn movies hidden there.
Worse: You're in them.

Good: Your husband understands fashion.
Bad: He's a cross-dresser.
Worse: He looks better than you do.

Good: Your son's finally maturing.
Bad: He is involved with the woman nextdoor.
Worse: So are you.

Good: You teach your daughter about the birds and the bees.
Bad: She keeps interrupting.
Worse: With corrections.

Good: Your wife's not talking to you.
Bad: She wants a divorce.
Worse: She's a lawyer.

Good: The postman's early.
Bad: He's wearing fatigues and carrying an AK-47.
Worse: You gave him nothing for Christmas.

GORILLAS

It's a beautiful, warm spring morning and a man and his wife are spending the day at the zoo. She's wearing a cute, loose fitting, pink spring dress, sleeveless and showing plenty of tit. As they walk through the ape exhibit, they pass in front of a very large hairy gorilla. Noticing the girl, the gorilla goes ape.

He jumps up on the bars, grunts and pounds his chest with his free hand. He is obviously excited at the pretty lady in the sexy dress. The husband, noticing the excitement, thinks this is funny. He suggests that his wife teases the poor fellow some more. The husband suggests she pucker her lips, stick her tits out and wiggle her bottom at him.

She does, and Mr Gorilla gets even more excited, making noises that would wake the dead. 'Now try lifting your dress up your thighs and sort of fan it at him,' her husband says. This drives the gorilla absolutely crazy and now he's doing flips.

Then the husband grabs his wife by the hair, rips open the cage, flings her in with the gorilla and slams the cage door shut.

'Now tell HIM you have a headache!'

A bloke wakes up one morning and finds a gorilla in his tree. He looks in the phone book and finds a gorilla removal service. When he asks if they can remove the gorilla they ask,

'Is it a male or a female?'

'Male,' he replies.

'Oh yeah, we can do it. I'll be right there,' he says.

An hour later , the service guy shows up with a stick, a chihuahua, a shotgun, and a pair of handcuffs. He then gives the man some instructions.

'I'm going to climb this tree and poke the gorilla with this stick until he falls out of the tree. When he does, the trained chihuahua will bite the gorilla's testicles off. The gorilla will then cross his hands to protect himself, allowing you to put the handcuffs on him.'

The man asks, 'What do I do with the shotgun?'

The service guy replies, 'If I fall out of the tree before the gorilla does, shoot the fucking chihuahua.'

GRANDPA'S 100th

Grandpa was celebrating his 100th birthday and everybody complimented him on how athletic and well-preserved he appeared.

'I will tell you the secret of my success,' he cackled. 'My wife and I were married 75 years ago. On our wedding night, we made a solemn pledge. Whenever we had a fight, the one who was proved wrong would go outside and take a walk. Gentlemen, I have been in the open air every day for some 75 years now.'

GRANDPARENTS
HOW TO TELL IF YOUR GRANDPARENTS ARE STILL HAVING SEX:

A pair of edible Depends found on the bedroom floor.

Lately they've been putting their teeth in the same glass.

Grandpa grabs his crotch and complains loudly of 'denture-burn'.

Granny is found cuffed to her walker.

You hear the bed squeaking, and also joints.

Grandma regularly looks at Grandpa's crotch and claps twice.
Grandma starts baking Viagra-chip biscuits.
Their automatic adjustable bed is set for 'doggy style'.

GRAVE GRIEF

A man placed some flowers on the grave of his dearly departed mother and started back toward his car when his attention was caught by another man kneeling at a grave. The man seemed to be praying with profound intensity and kept repeating, 'Why did you have to die? Why did you have to die?'

The first man approached him and said, 'Sir, I don't wish to interfere with your private grief, but this demonstration of pain is more than I've ever seen before. For whom do you mourn so deeply? A child? A parent?'

The mourner took a moment to collect himself, then replied, 'My wife's first husband.'

GRAVITY KILLS

A 22-year-old Melbourne man was found dead yesterday after he tried to use ockie straps (the stretchy little ropes with hooks on each end) to bungee jump off a 20-metre railroad trestle, police said. The fast-food worker had taped a bunch of these straps together, wrapped an end around one foot, anchored the other end to the trestle, jumped ... and hit the pavement. A police spokesman said investigators think he was alone because his car was found nearby. 'The length of the cord that he had assembled was greater than the distance between the trestle and the ground,' police said. The apparent cause of death was 'major trauma'.

GREAT MACHINES

A travelling salesman checked into a futuristic motel. Realising he needed a haircut before his next day's meeting, he called down to reception and asked if there was a barber on the premises.

'I'm afraid not, sir,' the receptionist told him, 'but down the hall is a special machine that should serve your purposes.'

Sceptical but intrigued, the salesman located the appropriate machine, inserted a dollar coin, and stuck his head in the opening, at which time the machine started to buzz and whirl. Fifteen seconds later the salesman pulled out his head and surveyed his head in the mirror. He saw the best haircut he had ever had in his life. Down the hall was another machine with a sign that read, 'Manicures — 30 cents.' 'Why not?' thought the salesman. He paid the money, inserted his hands into the slot, and pulled them out perfectly manicured.

The next machine had a huge sign that read, 'This Machine Provides What Men Need Most When

Away from Their Wives — cost 50 cents.'

The salesman was embarrassed and looked both ways. Seeing nobody around he put in a fifty cent piece, unzipped his pants, and stuck his penis into the opening — with great anticipation, since he had been away from his wife for two weeks.

When the machine started buzzing, the man let out a shriek of agony. Fifteen seconds later the machine shut off. With trembling hands, the salesman was able to withdraw his penis ...

... which now had a button sewed on the tip.

GYNAECOLOGIST

Jim's wife had a embarrassing appointment with the gynaecologist. She confessed, 'Early one morning I received a call from his office that I had been rescheduled for early that morning at 9.30. I had only just packed everyone off to work and school and it was around 8.45 already. The trip to his office usually took about thirty-five minutes so I didn't have any time to spare. As most women do I'm sure, I like to take a little extra effort over hygiene when making such visits but this time I wasn't going to be able to make the full effort so I rushed up stairs, threw off my dressing gown, wet the flannel and gave myself a wash in front of the basin taking extra care to make sure I was presentable. I threw the flannel in the wash basket, put on some clothes, hopped in the car and raced to my appointment.

'I was in the waiting room only a few minutes when he called me in. Knowing the procedure as I'm sure you all do, I hopped up on the table, looked over at the other side of the room and pretended I was a million miles away.

'I was a little surprised when he said, "My, we have taken a little extra effort this morning, haven't we?"

'The appointment over I heaved a sigh of relief and went home. The rest of the day went as normal, some shopping, cleaning, the evening meal, etc. That evening my 18-year-old daughter was fixing to go to a school dance when she called down from the bathroom, "Mum where's my flannel?" I told her to get another from the linen cupboard, but she called back, "No, I need my one that was here by the basin. It had all my glitter and sparkles in it."'

A Pitt Street gynaecologist took one look at a beautiful, voluptuous woman patient and all his professionalism went out the window. He told her to undress. After she had disrobed the doctor began to stroke her thigh. Doing so, he asked her, 'Do you know what I'm doing?'

'Yes,' she replied, 'You're checking for any abrasions or dermatological abnormalities.'

'That is right,' said the doctor.

Then he began to fondle her breasts. 'Do you know what I'm doing now?' he asked.

'Yes,' the woman said, 'You're checking for any lumps or breast cancer.'

'Correct,' replied the shady doctor.

Finally, he mounted his patient and started having sexual intercourse with her. He asked, 'Do you know what I'm doing now?'

'Yes,' she said. 'You're getting herpes, which is why I came here in the first place.'

H

HAIRY ARSE

A lawyer is driving in the middle of nowhere and his car breaks down. After waiting a while, a farmer comes along and asks what the problem is. Discovering the car couldn't be fixed easily or quickly, the farmer offers his home to the lawyer to stay for the night.

Later that night, the lawyer is asleep, and the farmer's wife comes in his room and wants to have sex with him. The lawyer says, 'No, you're husband will wake up and catch us.'

The wife replies, 'My husband is a heavy sleeper he won't wake up, I promise.' To prove it, she takes the lawyer into her room where her husband is naked and tells him to pull one of the hairs on his arse. The lawyer does and the farmer doesn't wake. They go back to the room and have sex.

About two hours later, the wife comes back and wants more. The lawyer says once again, 'Your husband will wake up and catch us.'

The wife says, 'I've already told you he's a heavy sleeper.' She takes him in her room again and he pulls another hair on the farmer's arse and still the farmer doesn't wake up. So they go out and have sex again.

It's almost sunrise and the wife comes back again and wants to do it one more time before her husband wakes up. The lawyer says, 'It's almost sunrise, he's about to wake up.'

The wife says 'Let me show you one more time that my husband is a heavy sleeper.' So they go back to her room and he pulls a hair on the farmer's arse.

Just then, the farmer turns around angrily, looks up at him and says: 'You can fuck my wife as many times as you want, but just don't use my arse as a scoreboard.'

HANGOVERS

Why are hangovers better than women?
Hangovers go away, and don't cost as much.

HE

He who does do what he is supposed to do,
for he he knows not who,
shouldn't do what he is doing,
for what he is doing may not be,
what he is supposed to be doing
for he he knows not who.

HEART ATTACK

A man came home from work early one day, and found his wife naked and panting on the bed.
 'Honey,' she said, thinking quickly, 'I think I'm having a heart attack!'

Rushing to call the doctor, he nearly stumbled over his crying four year old, who told him there was a naked man in the wardrobe.

He ran to the wardrobe, opened the door, and there was his best friend. 'For goodness sake, Dave'

he shouted, 'Jill's having a heart attack, and here you are scaring the kids to death!'

A middle-aged woman has a heart attack and is taken to the hospital. While on the operating table she has a near-death experience when she sees God. She asks Him if this is it. God says no and explains that she has another 30 years to live. Figuring that, since she's got another 30 years she might as well make the most of it, she decides to stay in the hospital and have a face lift, liposuction, breast augmentation, tummy tuck, and so on, and she even has someone come in and change her hair colour.

She walks out of the hospital after the last operation and is killed by an ambulance speeding up to the hospital.

When she gets to Heaven, she sees God and complains: 'I thought you said I had another 30 years?'

God replies, 'I didn't recognise you.'

HONEYMOON

A young couple were just married and they celebrated their first night together in a Surfer's Paradise highrise, doing what newlyweds do, time and time again, all night long. Morning comes and the groom goes into the bathroom but finds no towel when he gets out of the shower. He asks the bride to bring one from the bedroom. When she gets to the bathroom door, he opens the door, exposing his body for the first time to his bride.

Her eyes go up and down. About midway, they stop and stare and she asks, shyly, pointing to his drooping penis, 'What's that?'

He is also a bit shy, so he thinks for a moment, then says, 'Well, that's what we had so much fun with last night.'

And she, in amazement, says, 'Is that all we have left?'

HOW TO BE A WHACKER

- Wear socks with sandals.
- Wave at television cameras.
- Supply the punch lines to other people's jokes.
- Go to a party and talk about yourself, politics and religion.

🦜 Put expensive mag wheels on a car that rarely starts, often breaks down and belongs at the tip.

🦜 Read magazines only and no books.

🦜 Hang toys that wobble from the rear-view mirror of your car.

🦜 Drive with the radio on so loud that the whole street can hear it, even with the windows wound up.

🦜 Blame the system for your failures.

🦜 Wear T-shirts that say something like 'I love Hawaii' when the farthest you've ever been is Rosebud.

🦜 Light up a cigarette in a house with 'No Smoking Please' on the frontdoor.

🦜 Put catalogues, brochures, pamphlets in letter-boxes that say 'No junk mail please'.

🦜 Empty your coin jar with hundreds of 5 cent coins for counting by the bank teller, when the queue is out onto the street.

🦜 Pump up your tyres when there's a queue of cars waiting for petrol.

🦜 Order twelve beers, then try and pick all glasses up at once, instead of asking for a tray.

- Buy the *Financial Times*, then spend half an hour looking for the comics page.

- Ring someone at midnight, when you know that they always go to bed by 9.30 p.m.

- Repair broken reading glasses with bandaids, sticking plaster or cellotape.

- Take 49 items to the 8 item 'express lane' in a supermarket.

- Drive at slow speed in the right-hand lane of a freeway, often passing signs that say 'keep left unless overtaking'

- Whackers of the yuppie variety
  Spend money they don't have,
  on credit cards they can't afford,
  buying things they don't need,
  to impress people they really don't like.

HOW TO REFER TO WOMEN IF YOU WANT TO BE
POLITICALLY CORRECT

- She is not a BABE, CHICK
  — She is a BREASTED AUSTRALIAN.

- She is not a BLEACHED BLONDE
  — She is PEROXIDE DEPENDENT.

💋 She is not a BAD COOK
— She is MICROWAVE COMPATIBLE.

💋 She is not HALF NAKED
— She is WARDROBE IMPAIRED.

💋 She does not wear TOO MUCH JEWELRY
— She is METALLICALLY OVERBURDENED.

💋 She is not CONCEITED
— She is INTIMATELY AWARE OF HER BEST QUALITIES.

💋 She does not want to be MARRIED
— She wants to lock you in DOMESTIC INCARCERATION.

💋 She does not GAIN WEIGHT
— She is a METABOLIC UNDERACHIEVER.

💋 She is not a SCREAMER or MOANER
— She is VOCALLY APPRECIATIVE.

💋 She is not EASY
— She is HORIZONTALLY ACCESSIBLE.

💋 She does not TEASE or FLIRT
— She engages in ARTIFICIAL STIMULATION.

💋 She is not DUMB
— She is a DETOUR OFF THE INFORMATION SUPERHIGHWAY.

💋 She is not TOO SKINNY
— She is SKELETALLY PROMINENT.

- 💋 She does not HAVE A MOUSTACHE
  — She is IN TOUCH WITH HER MASCULINE SIDE.

- 💋 She does not HATE TELEVISED SPORTS
  — She is ATHLETICALLY IGNORANT.

- 💋 She has not BEEN AROUND
  — She is a PREVIOUSLY ENJOYED COMPANION.

- 💋 She does not WEAR TOO MUCH PERFUME —
  She commits FRAGRANCE ABUSE.

- 💋 She does not GET YOU EXCITED
  — She causes TEMPORARY BLOOD DISPLACEMENT.

- 💋 She is not KINKY
  — She is a NON-INHIBITED SEXUAL COMPANION.

- 💋 She does not have a KILLER BODY
  — She is TERMINALLY ATTRACTIVE.

- 💋 She does not GO SHOPPING
  — She is MALL FLUENT.

- 💋 She is not an AIRHEAD
  — She is REALITY IMPAIRED.

- 💋 She does not get DRUNK or TIPSY
  — She gets CHEMICALLY INCONVENIENCED.

- 💋 She does not get FAT or CHUBBY
  — She achieves MAXIMUM DENSITY.

- She is not COLD or FRIGID
  — She is THERMALLY INACCESSIBLE.
- She is not HORNY
  — She is SEXUALLY FOCUSED.
- She does not WEAR TOO MUCH MAKEUP
  — She has reached COSMETIC SATURATION.
- She does not have BREAST IMPLANTS
  — She is GRAVITY RESISTANT.
- She does not NAG YOU
  — She becomes VERBALLY REPETITIVE.
- She is not a SLUT
  — She is SEXUALLY EXTROVERTED.
- She is not LOOSE
  — She is MORALLY IMPAIRED.
- She does not have THICK LIPS
  — She is COLLAGEN DEPENDENT.

HOW?

How do you make a heap of old ladies yell 'shit' all at the same time?
Call out BINGO!

How many men does it take to screw in a light bulb?
One. Men will screw anything.

How many holes are there in half a crumpet?
About half as many as a full one.

How did the blonde burn her nose?
Bobbing for French fries.

How do you castrate a Tasmanian redneck?
You kick his sister in the jaw.

How do you find a blind man in a nudist colony?
It's not hard.

How do New Zealanders find sheep in long grass?
Very pleasurable

I

ICE CUBE

Two drunks are in a pub sitting at the bar, staring into their drinks. One gets a curious look on his face and asks, 'Hey, Pete, you ever seen an ice cube with a hole in it before?'

'Yes, I've been married to one for fifteen years.'

ICING ON THE CAKE

The was a little girl and her mother walking through the park one day and they saw two teenagers having sex on the bench.

The little girl says, 'Mummy, what are they doing?'

The mother hesitates, then quickly replies, 'Ummm, they are making cakes.'

The next day at the zoo the little girl sees two monkeys having sex. Again she asks her mother what they are doing and her mother replies with the same response — making cakes.

The next day the girl says to her mother, 'Mummy, you and daddy were making cakes in the living room last night, weren't you?'

Shocked the mother says, 'How do you know?'
The little girl says, 'Because I licked the icing off the sofa.'

IF

Blokes simply can't keep a woman happy:

If you stay home and do the housework, you're a pansy.
If you work too hard, there is never any time for her.
If you don't work enough, you're a good-for-nothing bum.
If she has a boring repetitive job with low pay, this is exploitation.
If *you* have a boring repetitive job with low pay, you should get off your bum and find something better.
If you get a promotion ahead of her, that is favouritism.
If she gets a job ahead of you, it's equal opportunity.

If you mention how nice she looks, it's sexual harassment.
If you keep quiet, it's male indifference.

If you cry, you're a wimp.
If you don't, you're an insensitive bastard.

If you thump her, it's wife bashing.
If she thumps you, it's self-defence.

If you make a decision without consulting her, you're a chauvinist.
If she makes a decision without consulting you, she's a liberated woman.

If you ask her to do something she doesn't enjoy, that's domination.
If she asks you, it's a favour.

If you appreciate the female form and frilly underwear, you're a pervert.
If you don't, you're a fag.

If you like a woman to shave her legs and keep in shape, you're sexist.
If you don't, you're unromantic.

If you try to keep yourself in shape, you're vain.
If you don't, you're a slob.

If you buy her flowers, you're after something.
If you don't, you're not thoughtful.

If you're proud of your achievements, you're up yourself.
If you don't, you're not ambitious.

If she has a headache, she's tired.
If you have a headache, you don't love her anymore.

If you want it too often, you're oversexed.
If you don't, there must be someone else.

INSULTS

You, from the shallow end of the gene pool.

Your mum and dad — are they brother and sister?
You're living proof evolution can work in reverse.
Smart as bait you are.
IQ of power tools.
Volvo owner.
He/she fell out of the stupid tree and hit every branch on the way down!
Couldn't organise a stink in a dunny!
Sharp as a bowling ball.
If brains were dynamite you couldn't blow your nose.

Twins with one head.
You've got the milkman's eyes.
100,000 sperm and you had to be the lucky one!
I can now see why some animals eat their young in the wild.
You have an IQ of 10. It takes 9 to grunt.

IRISH DRUNKS

There's an Irish rocket about to be launched to the sun,' said Paddy reading from a Dublin newspaper

'What about the heat; won't it melt?' asked Michael.

'No, it's leaving after dark,' says Paddy.

A man and woman were to be married but all members of both families appear in court.

The judge asks Paddy, the best man, to explain what happened.

'As you know,' says Paddy, 'It is traditional that the best man gets the first dance with the bride.'

The judge says, 'OK.'

'Well,' said Paddy, 'After I had finished the first dance, the music kept going, and we danced to the second song, and then into the third song, when all of a sudden the groom leapt over the table, ran towards us and kicked the bride right between her legs.'

Shocked, the judge instantly responded, 'Goodness, that must have hurt!'

'Hurt?' replies Paddy. 'I'll say! He broke three of my fingers!'

A drunken Irishman is driving through the streets of Adelaide on his way home from a pub and his car is weaving violently all over the road. A cop pulls him over.

'So,' says the cop to the driver, 'Where have you been?'

'I've been to the pub,' slurs the drunk.

'Well,' says the cop, 'it looks like you've had quite a few.'

'I did all right,' the drunk says with a smile.

'Did you know,' says the cop, standing straight and folding his arms, that a few intersections back, your wife fell out of your car?'

'Oh, thank heavens,' sighs the drunk. 'For a minute there, I thought I'd gone deaf.'

ITALIANS

You know you are Italian when:

You're 185 cm, can bench press 170 kilograms, shave twice a day, but still cry when your mother yells at you.

You carry your lunch in a fertiliser bag because you can't fit two mortadella and mozzarella 'sandwiches', four oranges, three bananas, a jar of olives, a foccaccio and a salami into a regular lunch box.

Your father owns two houses, has $100,000 in the bank, but drives a 1976 Monaro with pompom tassles around the windows, a crucifix hanging from the rearview mirror and the plastic still on the seats.

Your mother owns a house, has $100,000 in the bank but still believes she's entitled to the pension.

You share one bathroom with your five brothers and seven sisters, have no money, but drive a $75,000 Club Sport.

Your mechanic, plumber, electrician, accountant and travel agent are all blood relatives.

You consider dunking a pack of Teddy Bear bikkies in coffee a nutritious breakfast.

There are 30 pairs of slippers in your hall closet.

You live in a nine-square bungalow, but have two kitchens.

You have a $12,000 sound system in your 4-cylinder Gemini.

You wear a La Porchettas shirt and indoor soccer shoes to midnight mass.

Your two best friends are your cousin and brother-in-law's brother-in-law.

You own a tape that has Tony Bennett, Pearl Jam, and Ricki Martin on the same side.

You find it necessary to carry a pager despite the fact that you are a part-time produce clerk at Mario's fruit market.

You own a 'Ferrari Grand Prix' T-shirt from each of the last ten years.

Although you are at a disco four nights a week, you still can't drink more than two Ouzo-and-Cokes without wanting to pick a fight.

A favourite summer activity for you and your friends is sitting on the hood of your car blaring Tina Arena outside the local milk bar.

Despite the hair on your back, you still try to impress the ladies by wearing your 'Just do me' tank top to the local disco.

You know you're Calabrean or Sicilian when:

At least five of your cousins live on your street. All five are named after your grandfather.

You still wear see-through dress socks and pointy patent-leather dress shoes to weddings.

You are married and can still squeeze into your cream white confirmation suit.

There is a dump truck or tandem trailer in your life somewhere.

A high school diploma and a year of TAFE college has earned you the title of 'Professor' among your aunts.

You are on a first-name basis with at least ten banquet hall owners and green-grocers.

You have ten relatives named 'Maria' or 'Bruno'.

You have a tape with the dance version of 'Ave Maria' in your car.

It takes four disposable blades to shave your face.

If someone in your family grows beyond 170 cm, it is wondered whether your mother had an affair.

There are more than 28 people in your bridal party.

You netted more than $50,000 on your first communion.

Your father lives in a sub-division and still raises his own chickens and rabbits.

At some point in your life, you were a DJ or mowed the lawns at your uncle's.

You can name more people in the *Il Globo* obituaries than players on the Italia soccer team.

Thirty years after immigrating, your parents still say 'Pronto' when answering the phone.

You and your wife/husband have matching beanies for those cold winter mornings.

You are offended when the wedding you attend serves less than nine courses, despite the fact that you don't eat half of it.

You ask 'How much for cash?' when buying, but will accept 'gifts' in exchange for cash when selling.

You are not materialistic but insist a $500 wedding present is nothing.

You think your family is the next best thing to royalty and they have class, even though your parents didn't know what a refrigerator was until they arrived in Australia in the 1940s.

You think having swans in a big fountain in the front yard next to the vegie patch is tasteful.

You always have a friend who 'owes you a favour'.

You have concrete eagles and lion heads on your front fence, and whitewashed stones and a cactus as decoration.

You think having a concrete backyard is nice.

J

JACK

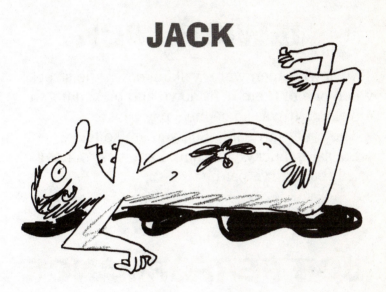

Once, in a small town, lived a man named Jack. Everyone in town knew Jack as a very optimistic person. Whenever he was in a terrible situation he would say, 'It could have been worse.'

Everyone in the town was tired of hearing this from Jack so one day they decided to lie to him. They went up to him and said, 'Jack, the baker Bob found his wife in bed with another man last night! He shot the man and then himself! Isn't it terrible?'

Jack replied, 'Well, yes it's terrible, but it could've been worse!'

The townspeople said, 'How could THAT possibly be worse?'

Jack said, 'Well, if it had been the night before I would've been dead!'

JEWISH LUCK

Two Jewish men were walking down the street when one of them bent down and picked up an envelope. It was someone's pay packet.

The other guy said, 'Sol, you are so lucky.

Sol said, 'Lucky, you think I am lucky? Just look at all the tax I've paid.'

JOB PERFORMANCE

If you work for a big company, you know what it's like when you get your performance review. But what do these terms really mean?

Average Employee: Not too bright.
Exceptionally Well Qualified: Made No Major Blunders Yet.
Active Socially: Drinks a lot.
Family Active Socially: Spouse drinks, too.
Character Above Reproach: Still one step ahead of the law.

Zealous Attitude: Opinionated.
Quick-Thinking: Offers plausible excuses.
Plans For Advancement: Buys drinks for all the boys.
Uses Logic On Difficult Jobs: Gets someone else to do it.
Expresses Themselves Well: Speaks in full sentences.
Meticulous: A nit picker.
Good Judgement: Lucky.
Career-Minded: Back-stabber.
Coming Along Well: About to be let go.
Of Great Value To The Organisation: Gets to work on time.
Relaxed Attitude: Sleeps at desk.
Work Is First Priority: Too ugly to get a date.
Independent Worker: Nobody knows what he/she does.
Forward Thinking: Procrastinator.
Great Presentation Skills: Able to bullshit.
Good Communication Skills: Spends lots of time on phone.
Loyal: Can't get a job anywhere else.
Keen Sense Of Humour: Knows a lot of dirty jokes.

JONAH

A little girl was observed by her pastor standing outside the pre-school Sunday School classroom between Sunday School and worship, waiting for her parents to come and pick her up for 'big church'. The pastor noticed that she clutched a big storybook under her arms with the obvious title, Jonah and the Whale.

He knelt down beside the little girl and began a conversation. 'What's that you have in your hand?' he asked.

'This is my storybook about Jonah and the whale,' she answered.

'Tell me something, little girl,' he continued, 'Do you believe that story about Jonah and that whale to be the truth?'

The little girl surprised replied, 'Why, of course I believe this story is true!'

He inquired further, 'You really believe that a man can be swallowed up by a big whale, stay inside him all that time, and come out of there still alive and OK? You really believe all that can be true?'

She declared, 'Absolutely, this story is in the Bible and we studied it in Sunday School today!'

Then the pastor asked, 'Well, little girl, can you prove to me that this story is true?'

She thought for a moment and then said, 'Well, when I get to Heaven, I'll ask Jonah.'

The pastor then asked, 'Well, what if Jonah's not in Heaven?'

She then put her hands on her little hips and sternly declared, 'Then YOU can ask him!'

K

KITCHEN

Why was the woman crossing the road?
Who cares; she shouldn't have been out of the bloody kitchen anyway.

KITTENS

A three-year-old went with his father to see a new litter of kittens. When he got home, he breathlessly told his mother that there were two boy kittens and two girl kittens.

'How did you know?' his mother asked.

'Daddy picked them up and looked underneath,' the child explained. 'I think it was printed on the bottom.'

KNEE TREMBLER

A couple have been married forty years and are revisiting the same places they went to on their honeymoon. As they are driving through the secluded countryside, they pass a farm with a tall deer fence running along the road.

The woman says, 'Sweetheart, let's do the same thing we did here forty years ago!'

The bloke stops the car and they get out. He backs her against the fence, and she immediately starts screwing him madly, moaning and groaning.

Back in the car, the bloke says, 'Dear, you never moved like that forty year ago — or any time since that I can remember.'

The woman says, 'Forty years ago that fence wasn't electrified!'

KNICKERS

A bloke walks into a bar and sits down next to this good looking girl and starts looking at his watch. The girl notices this and asks him if his date is late.

'No,' he replies, 'I've just got this new state-of-the-art watch and I was just about to test it.'

'What does it do?' she asked him.

'It uses alpha waves to talk to me telepathically.'

'What's it telling you now?'

'Well, it says you're not wearing any knickers.'

'Ha! Well, it must be knackered then 'cause I am!'

'Damn thing, must be an hour fast.'

L

LAUNDRY

Darling, what would I do without you?
Hopefully, the laundry — for the first time in your life!

LAWYERS

What's the difference between and sperm and a lawyer?
A sperm has a one in a million chance of becoming a human being ...

The scene is a dark jungle in Africa. Two tigers are stalking through the brush when the one to the rear reaches out with his tongue and licks the arse of the tiger in front.
　The startled tiger turns around and says, 'Hey! Cut it out.'
　The rear tiger says, 'Sorry,' and they continue.
　Five minutes later, the rear tiger again reaches out with his tongue and licks the arse of the tiger in front.

The front tiger turns around and cuffs the rear tiger and says, 'I said stop it!' The rear tiger says, 'Sorry,' and they continue.

After about another 5 minutes, the rear tiger once more licks the arse of the tiger in front. The front tiger turns around and asks the rear tiger, 'What is it with you, anyway?'

The rear tiger replies, 'Well, I just ate a lawyer and I'm trying to get the taste out of my mouth!'

A barber gave a haircut to a priest one day. The priest tried to pay for the haircut but the barber refused saying, 'I cannot accept money from you, for you are a good man — you do God's work.' The next morning the barber found a dozen Bibles at the door to his shop.

A policeman came to the barber for a haircut, and again the barber refused payment saying, 'I cannot accept money from you, for you are a good man — you protect the public.' The next morning the barber found a dozen doughnuts at the door to his shop.

A lawyer came to the barber for a haircut, and again the barber refused payment saying, 'I cannot accept money from you, for you are a good man you serve the justice system.' The next morning the barber found a dozen more lawyers waiting for a haircut.

LAWYER v. POLICE

A barrister was cross-examining a police officer during a felony trial — it went like this:

Q: Officer, did you see my client fleeing the scene?

A: No sir, but I subsequently observed a person matching the description of the offender running several blocks away.

Q: Officer, who provided this description?

A: The officer who responded to the scene.

Q: A fellow officer provided the description of this so-called offender. Do you trust your fellow officers?

A: Yes sir, with my life.

Q: With your life? Let me ask you this then officer — do you have a locker room in the police station — a room where you change your clothes in preparation for your daily duties?

A: Yes sir, we do.

Q: And do you have a locker in that room?

A: Yes sir, I do.

Q: And do you have a lock on your locker?

A: Yes sir.

Q: Now why is it, officer, if you trust your fellow officers with your life, that you find it necessary to lock your locker in a room you share with those officers?

A: You see sir, we share the building with a court complex, and sometimes the lawyers have been known to walk through that room.

In a long line of people waiting for a bank teller, one man suddenly started massaging the back of the person in front of him.

Surprised, the man in front turned and snarled, 'Just what the hell you are doing?'

'Well,' said the man, 'You see, I'm a chiropractor and I could see that you were tense, so I had to massage your back. Sometimes I just can't help practising my art!'

'That's the stupidest thing I've ever heard!' the man replied. 'I'm a lawyer. Do you see me fucking the guy in front of me?'

LAWYERS' DIRTY TALK

Have you looked through her briefs?
He is one hard judge!
Let's do it in chambers.
His barrister withdrew at the last minute.
Is it a penal offence?
Better leave the handcuffs on.
For $200 an hour, she'd better be good!
Can you get him to drop his suit?
The judge gave her the stiffest one he could.
Think you can get me off?

A man in a bar stands up and says, 'All lawyers are arseholes.'
Another man stands up and says 'Hey ... I resent that ...'
The first man says, 'Why? Are you a lawyer?'
The second man says, 'No. I'm an arsehole.'

LAXATIVE

Why is a woman like a laxative?
They both irritate the shit out of you.

LEGLESS

An Irishman's been drinking at a pub all night. The barman finally says that the bar is closing. So the Irishman stands up to leave and falls flat on his face. He tries to stand once more, same result. He figures he'll crawl outside and get some fresh air and maybe that will sober him up.

Once outside he stands up and falls flat on his face. So he decides to crawl the four blocks to his home. When he arrives at the door he stands up and falls flat on his face.

He crawls through the door into his bedroom. When he reaches his bed he tries again to stand up. This time he manages to pull himself upright but he quickly falls right into bed and is sound asleep as soon as his head hits the pillow.

He wakes up next morning to his wife standing over him shouting at him. 'So, you've been out drinking again!'

'What makes you say that?' he asks, putting on an innocent look.

'The pub called. You left your wheelchair there again.'

LEGS

Why do women have legs?
So they won't leave snail tracks.

LESBIANS

Nike have made a new shoe just for lesbians. It has a nine-inch tongue and cums off with one finger.

God create lesbians so the feminists couldn't breed.

What did the lesbian frog say to the other lesbian frog?
They're right! We do taste like chicken!

What do you call a truckload of dildos?
Toys for twats.

What did the banana say to the vibrator?
What are YOU shaking for? She's going to eat me!

What does a lesbian have in common with a mechanic?
Snap-on tools!

What do you call a lesbian with fat fingers?
Well-hung.

An innocent young man walks into a bar and notices two gorgeous young blondes seated near the end of the bar. He says to the barman: 'I'll have a beer and I'd like to buy those two ladies a couple of drinks.'

The barman smiles and says, 'I think you're wasting your time, mate. You see, they're lesbians.'

But the young man didn't understand and would not be put off, so the barman said, 'Look, why don't you go over there and ask them?'

So the young man walked over to the women and asked, 'I hear you are lesbians, what does that mean?'

One answered politely, 'Well, we like to kiss, suck each other's tits, and eat each other's pussy ...'

The young man turns and yells to the barman, 'Hey mate, bring three beers here for us lesbians, will you!'

How can you tell if lesbian carpenters built your house?
All the joints are tongue-in-groove and there are no studs.

LICKING

A group of friends were having a few quite ales when it was noticed one of the girls was missing. After a search, the police were called to report a possible kidnap. The police searched the venue and questioned patrons.

They then entered the manager's office only to find the girl tied naked in the manager's chair with his head between her legs.

The police were unable to lay charges as the bastard had a 'liquor licence'.

LIES

'The cheque is in the mail.'

'I'm not screwing your missus.'
(but my mate is)

'It won't hurt a bit.'

'I really like and respect you.'

'I'll ring you next week.'

'I know a good accountant.'
(there aren't any)

LIFE FROM A WOMAN'S PERSPECTIVE

Airhead: What a woman intentionally becomes when pulled over by a policeman.

Argument: A discussion that occurs when you're right, but he just hasn't realised it yet.

Bar-be-cue: You bought the groceries, washed the lettuce, chopped the tomatoes, diced the onions, marinated the meat and cleaned everything up, but he 'made the dinner'.

Blonde jokes: Jokes that are short so men can understand them.

Clothes drier: An appliance designed to eat socks.

Diet drink: A drink you buy at a convenience store to go with a kilo of M&M chocolate-covered peanuts.

Eternity: The last two minutes of a football game.

Exercise: To walk up and down a mall, occasionally resting to make a purchase.

Hair dresser: Someone who is able to create a style you will never be able to duplicate.

Hardware store: Similar to a black hole in space ... if he goes in, he isn't coming out soon.

Childbirth: You get to go through 36 hours of contractions; he gets to hold your hand and say, 'Focus ... breathe ... push ... good girl!'

Park: BC (before children) a verb meaning, 'to go somewhere romantic'. AC (after children) a noun meaning a place with a swing set and slide.

Patience: The most important ingredient for dating, marriage and children.

Valentine's Day: A day when you have dreams of a candlelight dinner, diamonds, and romance, but consider yourself lucky to get a card.

Waterproof mascara: Comes off if you cry, shower or swim, but will not come off if you try to remove it.

Zillion: The number of times you ask someone male to take out the trash, then end up doing it yourself anyway.

LIFE

Life wasn't meant to be easy.
— Malcolm Fraser, prime minister 1975–83

In all my life I have treated the press with marked contempt and remarkable success.
— Bob Menzies (1894–1978), prime minister 1939–41, '49–66

Life is mostly froth and bubble,
Two things stand like stone.
Kindness in another's trouble,
Courage in your own.
— Adam Lindsay Gordon (1833–79), Australian poet

LIGHT BULB

How many men does it take to change a light bulb?
None. They wait until the wife has finished the dishes in the kitchen.

How many women are needed to change a light bulb?
None. They just sit in the dark and bitch.

LINGERIE

The modest young lass had just bought some lingerie and asked if she might have the sentence, 'If you can read this you're too damn close' embroidered on her panties and bra.
 'Yes madam,' said the clerk. 'I'm quite confident

that could be done. Would you prefer block or script letters?'

'Braille,' she replied.

LINGO

ACCOUNTANT — Mongrel, Prick, Turd, Bastard
BANK MANAGER — Mongrel, Prick, Turd, Bastard
BUILDER — Chippie, Woodchip, 4by2
BUTCHER — Meat Muncher
DENTIST — Fang Farrier
DOCTOR — Quack, Sawbones
ELECTRICIAN — Sparkie
FARMER — Cockie, Dad'n'Dave

IDIOT — Mental Midget
MECHANIC — Grease Monkey
PAINTER — Two stroke
PLUMBER — S-Bend, Turd Strangler
POLITICIAN — Absolute 100% Lying Mongrel, Prick, Turd, Bastard
REAL ESTATE AGENT — Mongrel, Prick, Turd, Bastard
SCHOOL TEACHER — Shithead, Arsehole with Arrogance
WHARFIES — Sir.

As ugly as a hat full of arseholes
As cunning as a shithouse rat
Bangs like a dunny door in a gale
Dry as a dead dingo's balls

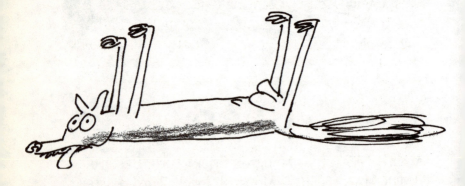

Dry as chips
Dry as a wooden God
Dry as a nun's nasty
Dry as an old Arab's fart
Flat as a shit carters hat
Flat out like a lizard drinking.

Happy as a pig in shit
Off like a rotten chop
Off like a herd of turtles
Off like a old mole's drawers
Off like a bride's nightie
Off like a Jew's foreskin
She's got a head like a smacked arse.
The bigger the Cushion, the better the Pushin'
The bigger the Rump, the better the Hump
You're about as handy as a half-open pocket knife.

LITTLE JOHNNIE

An old country doctor went way out to the remote outback to deliver a baby. It was so far out, there was no electricity. When the doctor arrived, no one was home except for the labouring mother and her 6-year-old son, little Johnnie. The doctor instructed little Johnny to hold a lamp high so he could see, while he helped the woman deliver the baby. The child did so, the mother pushed and after a little while, the doctor lifted the newborn baby by the feet and spanked him on the bum to get him to take his first breath.

The doctor then asked little Johnnie what he thought of his new baby brother.

'Hit him again,' said little Johnnie. 'The little bugger shouldn't have crawled up there in the first place!'

The first-grade teacher was starting a new lesson on multi-syllable words. She thought it would be a good idea to ask a few of the children for examples of words with more than one syllable.

'Jane, do you know any multi-syllable words?'

After some thought Jane proudly replied, 'Monday.'

'Great, Jane, that has two syllables, Mon-day.'

'Does anyone know another word.'

'I do, I do, me me me,' replied Johnnie.

Knowing Johnnie's more mature sense of humour, she picks Mike instead.

'OK Mike, what is your word?'

'Saturday,' says Mike.

'Great, that has three syllables.'

Not wanting to be outdone, Johnnie says, 'I know a four-syllable word, pick me …'

Not thinking he could do any harm with a word that large, the teacher reluctantly says, 'OK, Johnnie, what is your four-syllable word?'

Johnny proudly says, 'Mas-tur-ba-tion.'

Shocked, the teacher tries to keep her composure and says, 'Wow, Johnnie, four syllables, that certainly is a mouthful.'

'No teacher, you're thinking of "blowjob", and that's only two syllables.'

Little Johnnie came home from school one day and said, 'Mum, I learned a new word today; want me to tell it to you.'

Mum thought, 'Oh no, this will be good.' So she

asked, 'What letter does it start with, Johnnie?'

'M.'

Mum breathes a sigh of relief, 'OK, you can tell me the word.'

'Fuck'm,' said Johnnie.

A young teacher was giving an assignment to her Grade 6 class one day. It was a large assignment so she started writing high up on the blackboard. There was a giggle from one of the boys.

She turned around and asked, 'What's so funny Peter?'

'Well teacher, I just saw one of your garters.'

'Get out of my classroom,' she shouted, 'I don't want to see you for three days.' She turned back to the blackboard. Realising she had forgotten to give the assignment a title, she reached to the very top of the board.

There was an even louder giggle from another boy. She quickly turned and asked, 'What's so funny Mike?'

'Well teacher, I just saw both of your garters.'

Again she shouted, 'Get out of my classroom!' This time the punishment is more severe, 'I don't want to see you for three weeks.'

Embarrassed and frustrated, she drops the eraser when she turns around again. She bends over to pick it up. This time there is an all-out laugh from another male student.

She quickly turns to see little Johnnie leaving the classroom.

'Where do you think you are going, Johnnie?' she asks.

'Well teacher, from what I just saw, my school days are over!'

Little Johnnie's kindergarten class was on an excursion to their local police station where they saw posters, tacked to a bulletin board, of the Ten Most Wanted men. One of the youngsters pointed to a picture and asked if it really was the photo of a wanted person.

'Yes,' said the policeman. 'The detectives want him very badly.'

So, little Johnny asked, 'Why didn't you keep him when you took his picture?'

Little Johnnie was excited about his first day at school. So excited in fact, that only a few minutes after class started, he realised that he desperately needed to go to the toilet. He raised his hand politely to ask if he could be excused. Of course the teacher said yes, but asked Johnnie to be quick.

Five minutes later Johnnie returned, looking more desperate and embarrassed. 'I can't find it,' he said.

The teacher sat Johnnie down and drew him a little diagram to where he should go and asked him if he would be able to find it now. Johnnie looked at the diagram, said 'Yes' and went on his way.

Well, five minutes later he returned to the classroom and says to the teacher, 'I can't find it'.

Frustrated, the teacher asked Billy, a boy who has

been at the school for a while, to help him find the toilet.

So Johnnie and Billy go together. Five minutes later they both return and sit down at their seats.

The teacher asks Billy, 'Well, did you find it?'

Billy is quick with his reply: 'Oh sure, he just had his boxer shorts on backwards.'

A substitute teacher walks into the classroom. On the blackboard she sees a message. It says, 'Johnnie Poole, has got the biggest tool, in the whole damn school!'

Cross, she asks, 'Who's Johnnie Poole?'

This kid in the back stands up and says, 'I'm Johnnie Poole.'

'Well, Johnnie, you're staying after school!'

The very next day when the substitute teacher walks in, she looks up at the blackboard and written on it is the message, 'PAYS to ADVERTISE.'

It seems that a young couple had just got married and spent their wedding night with the young man's parents. In the morning the mother got up and prepared a lovely breakfast, went to the bottom of the stairs and called for them to come down to eat. After a long wait the family ate without the newly-weds.

The mother said 'I wonder why they never came down to eat.'

The groom's little brother, little Johnnie, said, 'Mum, I think …'

'Oh shut up, I don't want to hear what you think!' said the mother, not wanting to hear any inappropriate comments from the boy.

At lunch time she again prepared a wonderful meal and again called the young couple to eat. After another long wait the family proceeded to eat, and after the meal was over the mother once again said, 'I wonder why they never came down to eat?'

Once again little Johnnie started to speak, but was prevented by his mother.

At dinner time the mother cooked a very elaborate meal, set the table perfectly and called the newlyweds to join the family for dinner. After another long wait, she wondered out loud again why they had not come downstairs all day.

The boy again said, 'Mum, I think …'

'Well, what is it that you think?' asked the mother irritably.

'I think that when my big brother came down to get the vaseline last night, he got my model-plane glue instead.'

Husband and wife were screwing up a storm, after which the husband headed to the bathroom to clean up. He was halfway down the hallway when his son, little Johnnie, also stepped into the hallway. He was shocked to see his old man standing there wearing nothing more than a condom.

The boy pointed at his father's penis and asked, 'Dad, what are you doing?'

The father didn't want to start explaining about sex or birth control, so started a bullshit story, 'Son,

I'm trying to catch a mouse.'

The boy still in shock asked, 'What are you gonna do when you catch it ... FUCK IT?'

A third grade teacher came in to the room one day and found a drawing of a penis on the blackboard. She looked at her students suspiciously but didn't say anything. Instead, she rubbed it off.

Next day when she came into the classroom there was another drawing of a penis, this time twice as big. She didn't say anything, and quietly rubbed it off.

The next day when she came in she saw another drawing of yet an even bigger penis on the board. She frowned and rubbed it off.

The fourth day, she came in and saw another penis drawing. This time it's huge, covering almost the whole board. She couldn't take it any more, so she screamed at the room full of noisy children, 'Why do you kids like drawing this penis on the board? And why is it getting bigger each day?'

Little Johnnie answered back, 'The more you rub it, the bigger it gets.

Little Johnnie wakes up three nights in a row when he hears a thumping sound coming from his parents' bedroom. Finally one morning he goes to his mum and says, 'Mummy, every night I hear you and daddy making a noise and when I look in you're bouncing up and down on him.'

His mum is taken by surprise and says, 'Oh ... Well, I'm bouncing on his stomach because he's fat, and it makes him thin again.'

And the boy says, 'That won't work.'

His mum says, 'Why?'

'Because the lady nextdoor comes by after you leave each day and blows him back up!'

Little Johnnie's mother was in the shower when he walked in on her.

'Mum, what's that?' he said, pointing at her pubic hair.

'That's just my black sponge, Johnnie.'

Johnnie said nothing. A few days later he sees her

in the shower after she'd shaved it off.

'Mum, where's your black sponge?'

'Oh, I just lost it, now go and play.'

A few days later Johnnie came running into the kitchen, 'Mum, mum, I just found you black sponge?'

'Where, Johnnie?' said Mum, playing along with the joke.

'Mrs Johnson nextdoor is washing Dad's face with it!'

For homework little Johnnie had to interview a family member. He decided to interview his mother. He came home and said, 'Mum, I have to interview you for school.' She said OK and let him proceed to ask her questions. The first question was 'How much do you weigh?' The response was women don't say what they weigh. He said, 'OK' and asked 'How old are you?' His mother said, 'Women don't say how old they are.' She said, 'You can ask me one more question.' He said, 'Mum, why did your marriage fail?' She replied, 'That is none of your business. Go outside and interview some other people in the neighbourhood. I have things to do.'

Next day Johnnie comes home and says, 'Mummy, I got an A-plus on my homework.'

She says, 'Really. Who did you interview?'

Johnnie replies, 'You. Last night when you were asleep, I went through your wallet and got your driver's licence. You are 42, 80 kilos, and the reason your marriage failed was because you got an F in sex.'

One day, during a lesson on grammar, the teacher asked for a show of hands for who could use the word 'beautiful' twice in the same sentence.

First, she called on little Susie, who responded with, 'My father bought my mother a beautiful dress and she looked beautiful in it.'

'Very good, Susie,' replied the teacher. She then called on little Michael.

'My Mummy planned a beautiful banquet and it turned out beautifully,' he said.

'Excellent, Michael!' Then the teacher called on little Johnnie.

'Last night, at the dinner table, my sister told my father that she was pregnant, and he said, "Beautiful, fucking beautiful!"'

Little Johnnie was playing with his new electric train in the living room, unaware that his mother was working in the kitchen listening.

She heard the train stop and her son said, 'All of you sons of bitches who want off, get the hell off now, 'cause this is the last stop! And all of you sons of bitches who are getting on, get on the train 'cause we're going down the tracks.'

The mother went in and told her son, 'We don't use that kind of language in this house. Now I want you to go to your room and you are to stay there for two hours. When you come out, you may play with your train, but I want you to use nice language.'

Two hours later, the son comes out of the bedroom and resumes playing with his train. Soon the train stopped and the mother heard her son say, 'All passengers who are disembarking the train, please remember to take all of your belongings with you. We thank you for riding with us today and hope your trip was a pleasant one. We hope you will ride with us again soon.'

She hears the little boy continue, 'For those of you just boarding, we ask you to stow all of your hand luggage under your seat. Remember, there is no smoking on the train. We hope you will have a pleasant and relaxing journey with us today.'

The mother began to smile and a little tear came to her eye. She thought her son was so nice. Unexpectantly, little Johnnie calls out, 'For those of you who are pissed off about the two-hour delay, please see the fucking bitch in the kitchen.'

LITTLE KISS

Four strangers travelled together in the same compartment of a train. Two men and two women faced each other. One woman was a very wealthy and sophisticated 70-year-old who was decked out in the finest furs and jewelry. Next to her sat a beautiful young woman, 19 years old who looked like something off the cover of a fashion magazine. Across from the older woman was a very mature looking man in his mid-forties who was a highly decorated sergeant major in the army. And next to the sergeant major sat a young private fresh out of training camp.

As these four strangers travelled, they talked and chatted about trivial things until they entered an unlighted tunnel. There they sat in complete darkness and total silence, until the sound of a distinct kiss broke the silence. Following the kiss a loud slap could be heard throughout the cabin.

The four strangers sat quietly, thinking their own thoughts. The older lady was thinking, 'Isn't it wonderful that even in this permissive day and age there are still young women who have a little self-respect and dignity?' The young woman, shaking her head and greatly puzzled, asked herself, 'Why in the world would any man in his right mind want to kiss an old fossil like that when I'm sitting here?' The sergeant major, rubbing his sore face, was outraged that any woman could ever think that a man in his position would try to sneak a kiss in the dark.

And the private, grinning from ear to ear, was thinking, 'What a crazy mixed up world this is when a private can kiss the back of his hand and then smack a sergeant major in the face and get away with it!'

LOVE

What is love?
The delusion that one woman is different to another.

M

MACHO MEN

It is not that I fear death, I fear it as little as to drink a cup of tea.
— Ned Kelly (1855–80), bushranger

*

Balmain boys don't cry.
— Neville Wran, premier of NSW 1976–87

*

MAGICIAN

A magician is hired to entertain passengers on a long ship voyage. The first night, he starts his show in the lounge in front of an enthusiastic (if captive) audience. He has just produced a pack of cards from nowhere, and is about to take his bow, when the ship's parrot, in a cage but also in the lounge, squawks, 'I saw what you did! You pulled those from up your sleeve!' There is laughter and derision from the audience.

The next night the magician was opening with another trick, hiding a coin and making it reappear. As he prepared to take his bow, the blasted parrot squawked again, 'I saw that! You hid that in your shoe!' You guessed it, same response from the audience.

The magician had had enough! He went to the captain and said, 'That parrot! The little bird is ruining my show! Please do something about it!'

The captain managed to calm him down and came up with a simple solution — covering the cage! So, the show went on the next night, and just as the magician was pulling the rabbit from his hat, the ship hit a reef and sank. The magician was the only survivor.

After a couple of days floating on his raft, what should float by, but the cage, enveloped in a blanket! The magician ripped off the blanket. The parrot sat in the cage, blinked several times in the light and turned his head slowly from one side to another while looking around in a puzzled manner. 'All right,' said the parrot, 'I give up — where did you hide the ship?'

MALLEE ROOT

What's so damn good about a mallee root?
It's 30% hotter and goes 30% longer.

MARRIAGE

I married Miss Right. I just didn't know her first name was Always.

What is it called when a women is paralysed from the waist down?
Marriage!

It is not true that married men live longer than single men. It just seems a lot longer

MASTURBATION

More male lingo: wank, wanking, pull the pud, pump percy, throttle the ferret, bop the baloney, choke the chicken, hum the knob, squeezing the tomato, buffing the banana, shaking bacon, pounding on the flounder, mayonnaise making, spank the frank, wax the carrot.

Do you know what a Yankee is?
Same as a quickie, except you're by yourself.

MATHEMATICIAN

Colleen from Croydon and Debbie from Dromana were sitting having lunch and a ciggy in the Mall. Colleen looked into the distance. 'Gees, my life is so complicated I must be a mathematician?' she sighed.

Debbie looked at her 'What do you mean? Mathematician.'

'Well, says Colleen as she takes a drag. 'I keep trying to subtract from my weight, I'm always trying to add to my income, I'm always dividing my time, and always avoiding multiplying.'

MEMORABLE EVENTS

A western reporter goes to Serbia to write articles about that land. He meets an old man in a village and asks him about any memorable events in his life. The old man says, 'Well, one time my donkey got lost, so me and my neighbours got some vodka and went looking for it. We looked and looked and finally found the donkey. Then we drank the vodka and one by one started screwing the donkey; it was a lot of fun.'

The reporter figured he can't write an article about that, so he asked the old man to tell him another story. The old man said, 'Well, one time my neighbour's wife got lost, so me and all the village men got some vodka and went out looking for her. We looked and looked and finally we found her.

Then we drank the vodka and one by one screwed the neighbour's wife. It was a lot of fun.'

The reporter, feeling frustrated, told the old man that he couldn't write articles about those stories and asked him if he had any dramatic or sad memories that he *could* talk about. The old man paused a little and with a sad expression on his face said: 'Well, one time I was lost …'

MEN ARE LIKE:

Men are like … Place mats.
They only show up when there's food on the table.

Men are like … Mascara.
They usually run at the first sign of emotion.

Men are like … Bike helmets.
Handy in an emergency, but otherwise they just look silly.

Men are like … Government bonds.
They take so long to mature.

Men are like … Parking spots.
The good ones are taken, and the rest are too small.

Men are like … Copiers.
You need them for reproduction, but that's about it.

Men are like … Lava lamps.
Fun to look at, but not all that bright.

Men are like … Bank accounts.
Without a lot of money, they don't generate much interest.

Men are like … High heels.
They're easy to walk on once you get the hang of it.

Men are like … Curling irons.
They're always hot, and they're always in your hair.

Men are like … Mini skirts.
If you're not careful, they'll creep up your legs.

Men are like ... Bananas.
The older they get, the less firm they are.

MEN ARE NOT LIKELY TO SAY:

Stuff the football replay, let's go to the flower show instead.

While I'm up, can I get you a beer dear?

Sure, I'd love to wear that condom.

You're right, dear, you do know how to read a Gregory's.

You're right, her tits are just too big.

MEN WOULD PROBABLY SAY:

Don't worry; anal sex doesn't hurt.

Just swallow it, it won't choke you, and you'll like the taste.

MEN EXAGGERATE:

The size of their dick.

How many woman they've laid.
How important they are.
How many beers they can skoll.
The size of fish they've caught.

How much money they make.
What they own.
How much women can't live without them.
All the important people they know.
All the things they've done, and what they're going to do.

MEN FIRST

Call men what you want but it's true to say that men were:

FIRST to be created
FIRST to drive
FIRST to fly
FIRST to go into space
FIRST to walk on the moon
FIRST to climb Mount Everest
FIRST to invent almost bloody anything
FIRST to excell at almost everything
FIRST to sail the oceans
FIRST to explore and name most things on land sea and air
FIRST to go to war
FIRST to sign for peace
FIRST to finance
And FIRST to Fart
(OK, we're not sure about the last one!)

MEN HATE

Shitty nappies
Tampons
Women farting
Women who do silent but deadly farts
Bra clips
Girdles (passion killers)
Daggy knickers
Hairy legs and armpits (unless you're a Greek)
Work (unless you're a Jew)
Poofters (unless you're a poofter)

MEN LOVE

Big tits
Nice arses
Legs
Pretty faces
All of the above especially if they are on the same woman
Sport
Sex

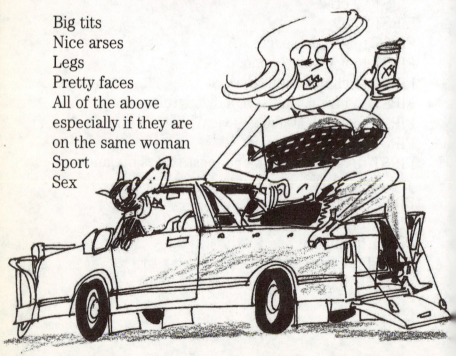

MEN ALSO LOVE

Grog
Cars, utes, motorbikes
Adventure
Mates
Sheds
Themselves

MEN v. WOMEN

A man will pay $2 for a $1 item he wants.
A woman will pay $1 for a $2 item that she doesn't want.

A woman worries about the future until she gets a husband.
A man never worries about the future until he gets a wife.

A successful man is one who makes more money than his wife can spend.
A successful woman is one who can find such a man.

To be happy with a man you must understand him a lot and love him a little.
To be happy with a woman you must love her a lot and not try to understand her at all.

Married men live longer than single men — but married men are a lot more willing to die.

Any married man should forget his mistakes — there's no use in two people remembering the same thing.

Men wake up as good-looking as they went to bed. Women somehow deteriorate during the night.

A woman marries a man expecting he will change, but he doesn't.
A man marries a woman expecting that she won't change and she does.

A woman has the last word in any argument. Anything a man says after that is the beginning of a new argument.

There are two times when a man doesn't understand a woman — before marriage and after marriage.

A mother takes twenty years to make a man of her boy, and another woman can make a fool of him in twenty minutes.

MEN WORDS

Men have a way with words. How many times have you heard a man, when asked if they wanted a cuppa tea or a cold beer, reply:

Do birds blink?
Do sparrows fart?
Do birds sing?
Do dachsunds' doodles dangle in the dirt?

Is the pope a catholic?
Is the bishop a catholic?

Is Rover a dog?
Does the pope wear a pointy hat?
Do penguins have cold arses?
Is the name Edward Woodward slightly repetitive?
Do convents have nuns? Do nun's have candles and do candles have batteries?
Is Plucka a duck?

MENSTRUATION

God gave it to all women as a curse for Eve luring Adam with the apple.
It just goes to prove God does have a sense of humour.

MIDGET AND HORSE

A man owns a horse stud farm and gets a call from a friend. 'I know this midget with a speech impediment who wants to buy a horse. I'm sending him over.'

The midget arrives, and the owner asks if he wants a male or female horse. 'A female horth,' the midget replies.

So the owner shows him one.

'Nith looking horth, can I thee her mouth?' So the owner picks up the midget and shows him the horse's mouth.

'Nith mouth. Can I thee her eyesth?' So the owner picks up the midget and shows him the eyes.

'OK, what about her earth?' Now the owner is

getting pissed, but he picks up the midget one more time and shows him the ears.

'OK, finally, I'd like to thee her twat.' With that, the owner picks up the midget and shoves his head up the horse's canal, then pulls him out.

Shaking his head, the midget says, 'Perhapth I should rephrase. I'd like to thee her run!'

MIRACLE

A woman starts dating a doctor. Before too long, she becomes pregnant and they don't know what to do. About nine months later, just about the time she is going to give birth, a priest goes into the hospital for a prostate gland operation. The doctor says to the woman, 'I know what we'll do. After I've operated on the priest, I'll give the baby to him and tell him it was a miracle.'

'Do you think it will work?' she asks the doctor.

'It's worth a try,' he says. So, the doctor delivers the baby and then operates on the priest. After the operation he goes in to the priest and says, 'Father, you're not going to believe this.'

'What?' says the priest. 'What happened?'

'You gave birth to a child.'

'But that's impossible!'

'I just did the operation,' insists the doctor. 'It's a miracle! Here's your baby.'

About fifteen years go by, and the priest realises he must tell his son the truth. One day he sits the boy down and says, 'Son, I have something to tell you. I'm not your father.'

The son says, 'What do you mean, you're not my father?'

The priest replies, 'I'm your mother. The archbishop is your father.'

MISTRESS

A married couple was enjoying a dinner out when a statuesque brunette walked over to their table, exchanged warm greetings with the husband, and walked off.

'Who was that?' the wife demanded.

'If you must know,' the husband replied, 'that was my mistress.'

'Your mistress? That's it! I want a divorce!' the wife fumed.

The husband looked her straight in the eye and said, 'Are you sure you want to give up our big house in the suburbs, your Mercedes, your furs, your jewelry, and our holiday house at Noosa?'

For a long time they continued dining in silence. Finally, the woman nudged her husband and said, 'Isn't that Howard over there? Who's he with?'

'That's HIS mistress,' her husband replied.

'Oh,' she said, taking a bite of dessert. 'Ours is much cuter.'

MOTHER-IN-LAW

One day, a farmer's mother-in-law came down to his farm. A few days later, a pig on the farm bit her, and she died of blood poisoning.

Hundreds of people from town who had heard about the death came to the poor woman's funeral, some that the farmer didn't even know. A minister noticed this, came up to the farmer, and asked, 'Why are there so many people here?'

The farmer answered, 'Oh, they're not here for the funeral, they want to buy the pig.'

N

NAGGER

Hitting on the novel idea that he could end his
wife's nagging by giving her a good scare, Jack built

an elaborate harness to make it look as if he had hanged himself. When his wife came home and saw him, she fainted. Hearing a disturbance a neighbour came over and, finding what she thought were two corpses, seized the opportunity to loot the place. As she was leaving the room, her arms laden, the outraged and suspended Jake kicked her stoutly in the backside. This so surprised the lady that she dropped dead of a heart attack. Happily, Jake was acquitted of manslaughter and he and his wife were reconciled.

NAKED

An unidentified woman was climbing into the bathtub one afternoon when she remembered she had left some muffins in the oven. Naked, she dashed downstairs and was taking the muffins out of the oven when she heard a noise at the door. Thinking it was the baker, and knowing he would come in to leave the bread on the kitchen table if she didn't answer his knock, the woman darted into the broom cupboard.

A few moments later she heard the back door open and, to her eternal mortification, the sound of footsteps coming toward the cupboard. It was the man from the gas company, come to read the meter, which was inside the broom cupboard.

'Oh,' stammered the woman, 'I was expecting the baker.' The gas man blinked, excused himself and departed.

NAMES

A pregnant woman from Adelaide has a car accident and falls into a deep coma. Asleep for nearly six months, when she wakes up she sees that she is no longer pregnant and frantically asks the doctor about her baby.

The doctor replies, 'Ma'am you had twins! A boy and a girl. Your brother from Tasmania came and named them.'

The woman thinks to herself, 'Oh no, not my brother — he's an idiot!' She asks the doctor, 'Well, what's the girl's name?'

'Denise.'

'Wow, that's not a bad name, I like it! What's the boy's name?'

'Denephew.'

The manager of a large office in Darwin noticed a new man one day and told him to come into his office. 'What is your name?'

'John,' the new guy replied.

The manager scowled, 'Look, I don't know what kind of a place you worked at before, but I don't call anyone by their first name. It breeds familiarity and that leads to a breakdown in authority. I refer to my employees by their last name only — Smith, Jones, Baker — that's all. I am to be referred to only as Mr Robertson. Now that we've got that straight, what is your last name?'

The new guy sighed and said, 'Darling. My name is John Darling.'

'OK, John, the next thing I want to tell you is ...'

NEIGHBOURS

On the sixth day God turned to the angel Gabriel and said, 'Today I am going to create a land called Canada. It will be a land of outstanding natural beauty. It will have tall majestic mountains full of mountain goats and eagles, beautifully sparkling lakes bountiful with carp and trout, forests full of elk and moose, high cliffs overlooking sandy beaches with an abundance of sea life, and rivers stocked with salmon.

'I shall make the land rich in oil so to make the inhabitants prosper. I shall call these inhabitants Canadians. They will be known as the friendliest people on the earth.'

'But Lord,' asked Gabriel, 'Don't you think you are being too generous to these Canadians?'

'Not really,' replied God, 'Just wait and see the neighbours I am going to give them!'

NEW COURSES FOR WOMEN

The following training courses are now available for women:

1. Silence, The Final Frontier: Where No Woman Has Gone Before
2. The Undiscovered Side Of Banking: Making Deposits
3. Combating Imelda Marcos Syndrome: You Don't Need New Shoes Every Day
4. Parties: Going Without New Outfits
5. Man Management: Discover How Minor Household Chores Can Wait Until After The Game
6. Bathroom Etiquette 1: Men Need Space In The Bathroom Cabinet Too
   Bathroom Etiquette 2: His Razor Is His
7. Communication Skills 1: Tears - The Last Resort, Not The First
   Communication Skills 2: Thinking Before Speaking
   Communication Skills 3: Getting What You Want, Without Nagging
8. Driving A Car Safely: A Skill You Can Acquire
9. Party Etiquette: Drinking Your Fair Share
10. Telephone Skills: How To Hang Up
11. Introduction to Parking
12. Introduction to Petrol
13. Advanced Parking: Reversing Into A Space
14. Advanced Petrol: Taking the Filler Cap Off

15 Water Retention: Fact or Fat
16 Cooking 1: Bran And Tofu Are Not For Human Consumption
   Cooking 2: How Not To Inflict Your Diet On Other People
17 PMS: Your Problem — Not His
18 Dancing: Sober Men Don't Like To
19 Sex — It's For The Married Couple Too
20 Classic Clothing: Wearing Clothes You Already Have
21 Household Dust: A Harmless Natural Occurrence Only Women Notice
22 TV Remotes: For Men Only
23 Bathrooms: They Do Look The Same Before And After Cleaning
24 Unisex Shopping: What You Spend On Clothes I Am Allowed To Spend On Beer, Since I Will Have The Beer Inside Me For About The Same Time You Will Wear The Clothes

NIPPLES

Why did God give women nipples?
To make suckers out of men.

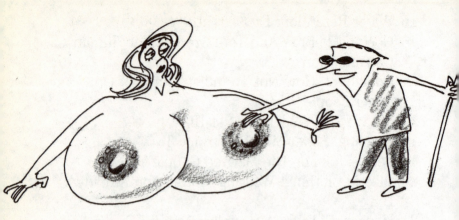

What are the small bumps around a woman's nipple for?
It's braille for 'suck here'.

NORM

Ralph and his wife Beryl were walking down the street when Ralph spotted an old War mate. 'Norm,' cried Ralph. 'Gees, haven't seen you for years. Beryl, this is Norm. He saved my life on Kokoda; he even donated me a kidney. Ah, mate you were always the best.'

They invited Norm home for tea. They were about to sit down to a wonderful dinner, when Ralph said, 'I'll just duck back up the street and grab a nice bottle of red for you Norm, mate.'

He returns to find his wife naked, flat on her back on the kitchen floor, with naked Norm screwing her madly.

'Oh Jesus, Beryl,' he says, 'How could you. At least arch your back, so Norm's balls are off the cold lino floor.'

NOT AMUSED

A Frenchman, a German and an Englishman are in the pub. The Frenchman says, 'Last night I poured cognac all over my wife, licked it off and made love to her for three hours. She rose half a metre off the bed.'

The German says, 'That's nothing. Last night I smothered my wife with sauerkraut, ate it all off and made love to her for four hours. She rose a full metre off of the bed.'

The Englishman says with a smirk, 'You light-weights — last night I got drunk, made love to my wife for two minutes, wiped my dick on her nightie, and called her a bitch. She hit the frigging roof!'

NUDIST

A man moves into a nudist colony. He receives a letter from his mother asking him to send her a current photo of himself in his new location. Too embarrassed to let her know that he lives in a nudist colony, he cuts a photo in half and sends her the top part.

Later he receives another letter asking him to

send a picture to his grandmother. The man cuts another picture in half, but accidentally sends the bottom half of the photo. He is really worried when he realises that he has sent the wrong half, but then remembers how bad his grandmother's eyesight is, and hopes she won't notice.

A few weeks later he receives a letter from his grandmother. It says, 'Thank you for the picture. Change your hair style … it makes your nose look too short!'

NUNS

Two nuns were riding bicycles down a laneway through the Rocks, an old part of Sydney.

'I haven't come this way before,' said one nun.

'Must be the cobblestones,' replied the other.

'Doctor, why is that nun in the waiting room crying like that?' says the nurse.

'Oh, I just told her she's pregnant.'

'Oh poor thing.'

'Actually, she isn't pregnant, but I've completely cured her hiccups!'

A nun is walking down a deserted road when a man grabs her and starts raping her. After the rapist is done, he says, 'Hey Sister, what are you going to tell the other Sisters now?'

'I'll tell them the truth, that you grabbed me, threw me to the ground, and raped me twice ... unless you're tired,' she responded.

Two nuns who have been working with Aborigines in the outback for many years come to Sydney and one says to the other, 'I hear that the people of this city actually eat dogs.'

'Odd,' her companion replies, 'But if we live in the city, we might as well do as the city people do.'

Nodding emphatically, the first nun points to a hot dog stand and they both walk towards the cart.

'Two dogs, please,' says one.

The vendor obliges, wrapping both hot dogs in foil and handing them over the counter. Excited, the nuns hurry over to a bench, sit down and begin to unwrap their dogs.

The first nun is first to open hers. She begins to blush and then, staring at it for a moment, leans

over to the other nun. She whispers cautiously, 'What part of the dog did you get?'

NUTS!

Bazza from Ballarat came home and caught his wife in bed with the nextdoor neighbour. He pulled his shotgun from the cupboard and burst into the bedroom. The bloke flew out of bed and backed up against the wall cowering.

Bazza aimed his shotgun at the neighbour's testicles. 'Right you prick, now I'm gonna blow your balls off.'

'Come on, mate. I'm a sitting duck. What about giving me a sporting chance?'

'OK, swing 'em, you bastard!'

OFFICE MEMORANDUM

It has been brought to management's attention that some individuals in the company have been using foul language during the course of normal conversation with their co-workers. This type of language will no longer be tolerated so we've evolved some guidelines:

PREFERRED: Perhaps I can work late.
OLD: When the fuck do you expect me to do this?

PREFERRED: I'm certain that is not feasible.
OLD: No fucking way.

PREFERRED: Really?
OLD: You've got to be shitting me.

PREFERRED: Of course I'm concerned.
OLD: Ask me if I give a shit.

PREFERRED: I wasn't involved in that project.
OLD: It's not my fucking problem.

PREFERRED: That's interesting behaviour.
OLD: What the fuck?

PREFERRED: I'm not sure I can implement this.
OLD: Fuck it, it won't work.

PREFERREDD: I'll try to schedule that.
OLD: Why the hell didn't you tell me sooner.

PREFERRED: So you weren't happy with it?
OLD: Kiss my arse.

!?!

PREFERRED: Are you sure this is a problem?
OLD: You stupid shit, not only do I think you don't understand diddly, I wouldn't give a shit if you did.

!?!

PREFERRED: He's not familiar with the problem.
OLD: He's got his head up his arse, what would make you think he'd know anything?

!?!

PREFERRED: I don't think you understand.
OLD: I'm tired of talking to you, you simple-minded fool, and if I have to explain myself again I will have to hurt you.

!?!

PREFERREDI love a challenge.
OLD: This job sucks and the suckage continues to escalate.

!?!

PREFERRED: I see.
OLD: Blow me.

!?!

PREFERRED: Yes, we really should discuss it.
OLD: Another fucking meeting.

!?!

PREFERRED: I don't think this will be a problem.
OLD: I'm overworked and underpaid therefore I really don't give a shit.

PREFERRED: He's somewhat insensitive.
OLD: He's a fucking prick.

!?!

PREFERRED: I think you could use more training.
OLD: You don't know what the fuck you're doing?

OLD BREASTS

What does a 75-year-old woman have between her breasts that a 25-year-old doesn't?
A navel.

This 65-year-old woman is naked, jumping up and down on her bed, laughing and singing. Her husband walks into the bedroom and sees her. He watches her a while, then says, 'You look ridiculous! What on earth do you think you're doing?'

She replies, 'I just got my check-up and my doctor says I have the breasts of an 18 year old.' She starts laughing and jumping again.

He says, 'Yeah, right. And what did he say about your 65-year-old arse?'

'Your name never came up …' she replied.

OLD MAN

A man asked his doctor whether he would live to be a hundred.

The doctor asked the man, 'Do you smoke or drink?'

'No,' he replied, 'I've never done either.'

'Do you gamble, drive fast cars, and fool around with women?' inquired the doctor.

'No, I've never done any of those things.'

'Well then,' said the doctor, 'What the hell do you want to live to be a hundred for?'

OLD MEMORY

An older man and his friend were having a conversation one night, and the topic drifted to memory, or lack of it. The first man says to his friend, 'My wife and I have been having a hard time remembering very simple things lately. A friend recommended that we see this memory specialist doctor.'

'Oh. Well, how is it working out for you?' asked the friend. 'Has it helped either one of your memories?'

'Very much so!' replied the man. 'The results are incredible!'

'What's the name of this doctor?' asked his friend.

'Hmm, it's a really long last name, I know,' he replied. 'Well, help me out for a second. What's the name of the kind of flower, the one with the thorns, that grows on a bush?'

'A rose?' said his friend.

'Yes, Yes! A rose!' says the man. 'Rose, dear, what's the name of that memory doctor we've been seeing?'

OLD MUM

Once upon a time, a mature woman in her sixties decided that she wanted to have a baby. She read all about the modern fertility procedures for older women. She decided that she would get pregnant, and have a baby. And she did, One of her old friends dropped by her house, and wanted to see the baby. She said, 'The baby is napping, and you'll have to wait until he wakes up.'

So they talked for a while. Then the friend said she had to go but she really did want to see the baby. The mother was quite adamant: 'You'll have to wait until he wakes up.'

The visitor said, 'Can't I just peek in and look at him sleeping?'

The mother admitted, 'I can't remember where I put him, but when he wakes up and cries, then I'll know where he is …'

OLD RAPIST

Two old men meet on a street corner.
First old man: 'Where have you been for the last couple of months?'
Second old man: 'I was in gaol.'
First old man: 'You were in gaol, how come?'
Second old man: 'Well, about two months ago I was standing on a corner, and this beautiful young woman rushes up with a policeman, points to me and says, "He is the man officer! He is the one who attacked and raped me."'
First old man: 'What! And you let her get away with it?'
Second old man: 'Well, I'll tell you, I felt so flattered, I admitted to it.'

OLD SEX

'I may be 87, but I make love nearly every night of the week with my Mabel,' says Harold.
  'That's bullshit, Harold, you're exaggerating,' said Fred.
  'No, I'm fair dinkum,' replies Harold. 'I nearly made it on Monday, I nearly made it on Tuesday, …'

ORAL SEX

How do you tell if a woman likes oral sex?
She lifts her skirt every time someone yawns.

ORGASMS

A farmer in Tasmania and his wife were lying in bed one evening. She was knitting; he was reading the latest issue of Animal Husbandry. He looks up from the page and says to her, 'Did you know that humans are the only species in which the female achieves orgasm?'

She looks at him wistfully, smiles, and replies, 'Oh yeah? Prove it.'

He frowns for a moment, then says, 'OK.' He then gets up and walks out, leaving his wife with a confused look on her face.

About half an hour later he returns all tired and sweaty and says, 'Well, I'm sure the cow and sheep didn't, but the way that pig squealed, it's hard to tell.'

PANTIES

What's the white stuff in women's panties?
Clitty litter.

PANTYHOSE

You can tell when a woman is wearing pantyhose because her ankles swell up when she farts.

Herbert met Flo in a bar one night and began buying her drinks. They hit it off pretty well and soon Bert suggested they go to his apartment for some rooting. Well, it wasn't long before they found themselves in bed making passionate love. As they were making love though, Bert noticed that Flo's toes would curl up as he was thrusting in and out. When they were done, Bert lay back on the bed and said, 'I must have been pretty good tonight. I noticed your toes curling up when I was going in and out.' Flo looked at him and smiled, 'That usually happens when someone forgets to remove my pantyhose.'

PARENT'S DREAM

An older couple had a son who was still living with his parents. The parents were a little worried as the son was still unable to decide about his career path. So they decided to do a small test. They found a $10 note, a Bible, and a bottle of whisky, and put them on the front hall table.

The father told the mother, 'If he takes the money he will be a businessman; if he takes the Bible he will be a priest; but if he takes the bottle of whisky, I'm afraid our son will be a drunkard.'

Then they hid in a nearby cupboard, hoping he would think they weren't at home, and waited nervously. Peeping through the keyhole they saw their son arrive home. He read the note they had left telling him they would be home later. Then he saw the $10 note, looked at it against the light, and slid it into his pocket. He picked the Bible up, flicked through it, and took it too. Finally, he grabbed the bottle, opened it, and took an appreciative whiff, assuring himself of the quality. He left for his room, carrying all three items.

The father slapped his forehead, and said: 'Damn, it's even worse than I imagined...'

'What do you mean?' his wife inquired.

'Our son is going to be a politician!' replied the concerned father.

PARROT TALK

A bird auction at a South Australian Parks and Wildlife depot attracted a large crowd. A couple were bidding for a sulphur-crested parrot, and they were clearly determined to get it. The man standing beside them couldn't believe how much they were bidding. The husband says to his wife. 'I can't believe how much this bird is costing me. I hope he is a good talker.'

The man standing beside them laughed and said, 'Don't worry, mate, he's a good talker all right. Who do you think has been bidding against you all this time?'

A woman was thinking about finding a pet to keep her company at home. She decided she would like a beautiful parrot. It wouldn't be as much work as a dog, and it would be fun to hear it talk.

She went to a pet shop and immediately spotted a large beautiful parrot. She found the owner of the store and asked how much the bird cost. The owner said $50.

Delighted that such a rare-looking and beautiful bird wasn't more expensive, she agreed to buy it.

The owner looked at her and said, 'Look, I should tell you first that this bird used to live in a whorehouse. Sometimes it says some pretty vulgar stuff.'

The woman thought about this, but decided she still wanted the bird, so the sale was agreed and she took it home. She hung the bird's cage up in her living room and waited for it to say something.

The bird looked around the room, then at her, and said, 'New house, new madam.'

The woman was a bit shocked at the implication, but then thought, 'That's not so bad.'

A couple of hours later, the woman's two teenage daughters returned from school. When they inspected the bird, it looked at them and said, 'New house, new madam, new whores.'

The girls and the woman were a bit offended at first, but then began to laugh about the situation.

A couple of hours later the woman's husband came home from work.

The bird looked at him and said, 'New house, new madam, new whores. Hi, Frank!'

PEARLY GATES

A man is at the pearly gates, waiting to be admitted, while St Peter is leafing through a Big Book to see if the man is worthy of entering. St Peter goes through the book several times, furrows his brow, and says to the man, 'You know, I can't see that you did anything really good in your life but, you never did anything bad either. Tell you what, if you can tell me of one REALLY good deed that you did in your life, you're in.'

The man thinks for a moment and says, 'Yeah, there was this one time when I was driving down the highway and I saw a giant group of Biker Gang Rapists assaulting this poor girl. I slowed down to see what was going on, and sure enough, there they were, about 50 of them torturing this girl. Infuriated, I got out of my car, grabbed a tyre iron out of my trunk, and walked straight up to the leader of the gang, a huge guy with a studded leather jacket and a chain running from his nose to his ear. As I walked up to the leader, the Biker Gang Rapists formed a circle around me. So, I rip the leader's chain off his face and smash him over the head with the tyre iron. Then I turn around and yell to the rest of them, "Leave this poor, innocent girl alone! You're all a bunch of sick, deranged animals! Go home before I teach you all a lesson in pain!"'

St Peter, impressed, says, 'Really? When did this happen?'

'Oh, about two minutes ago.'

PENIS

A man walks into a bar and sits down. The bartender says to him, 'Hey, look at this,' and he pulls a little piano out of his pocket.

'Hey, great,' says the man. 'Where did you get that?'

'No, wait, look at this!' says the bartender. And he pulls a little man out of his pocket, sits him at the little piano and he starts playing.

'Wow!' says the man. 'How did you get that?'

'Well', says the bartender, I was walking down the street one day and I found this,' he says, and pulls out a lamp. 'I rubbed and a genie popped out and told me I could have one wish.'

'Can I have a go?' asks the man.

He rubs the lamp and the genie pops out and says, 'You have one wish.'

So the man says, 'I wish for a million bucks!'

And lo and behold, a million ducks start flying around the bar. Once they had all cleared out, the man says, 'Hey, what's going on, I asked for a million bucks, not a million ducks!'

'Yeah,' says the bartender. 'Do you really think I'd ask for an 11-inch little man to play with?'

Why did God give men penises?
So we have at least one way to shut women up.

What is the most active muscle in a woman?
A penis.

A young woman experienced some car trouble late one afternoon but luckily an old man in a tow truck stopped and offered help.

Not knowing the area, she asked if he could repair the car. He agreed to do it, hoisted the car up on the truck, and the two of them towed the car back to the old man's garage.

There he looked at the engine and made an estimate of one hundred dollars, which was more than she had.

'Damn, I'm just one hundred dollars short of cash. If you weren't such an old guy,' she said, 'I'd screw you for the rest of the bill.'

'Hell, I'll show you whose old!' the old man retorted, 'Take off that dress and get on the car.'

She giggled as she slipped off her dress and eyed the old man after he dropped his pants. He was hung like a mule!

'Oh boy!' she thought. 'Not only am I going to get a great discount on the repairs, I'm going to get screwed out of my brains.'

Then she noticed the old man placing washers on the base of his pecker.

'Hey, what are you doing?' the woman asked.

'Hell,' the old man replied, 'You think for just a hundred dollars, you're going to get all of this?'

PENIS GRIP

What's the difference between red and purple?
Your grip.

PENIS PROBLEMS

A man is having problems with his penis, which certainly had seen better times. He consults a doctor who, after a couple of tests, says, 'Sorry, but you've overdone it the last 30 years. Your penis is burned out. You only have 30 erections left in your penis.'

The man walks home, deeply depressed.

His wife is waiting for him at the front door and asks him what the doctor said about his problem. He tells her what the doctor told him.

She says, 'Oh no, only 30 times! We shouldn't waste that. We should make a list!'

He replies, 'Yes, I've already made a list on the way home. Sorry, your name isn't on it.'

PERFECT PUT-DOWN

'I didn't attend the funeral, but sent a nice letter, saying I approved of it.'

— Mark Twain

PERIOD

Women are like oysters — because when the red tide comes you don't eat them.

What is the definition of a period?
A bloody waste of fucking time.

Why do women have periods?
Because they deserve them.

PIG

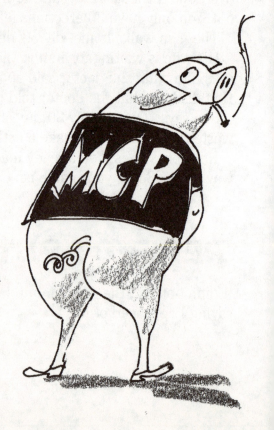

What is the definition of a male chauvinist pig?
A man who hates every bone in a woman except his own.

What's worse than a male chauvinist pig?
A woman who won't do as she is told.

A farmer was getting worried that his pigs weren't getting pregnant so he called a vet. The vet told him to try artificial insemination. Being stupid he thought this meant impregnating them himself. He loaded the pigs into his truck, drove into the woods, and shagged them all. He called the vet and asked how would he know if they were pregnant. The vet told him they would be lying down rolling in the mud. But next morning when he looked out of the window, all the pigs were standing up.

Once again he loaded them onto the truck, took them into the woods and shagged them. Next morning all the pigs were still standing up.

To his dismay this happened every day for a week.

Then one morning he was just too knackered even to look out of the window, so he asked his wife to check on the pigs for him.

'That's weird,' she said. 'All the pigs are in the truck, and one of them is beeping the horn ...'

PISSER

A guy walks into a bar. He sits down and says to the bartender, 'I'll bet you $100 that if you put a shot glass at that end of the bar, I could stand at the other end and fill it up with piss.'

Well the bartender thinks, 'That's an easy $100,' and says 'OK.'

So the guy gets on top of the bar and pees everywhere, even on the bartender. Well, the bartender doesn't care; he's just won $100. So very happily the bartender asks for his money. The guy also very happily says, 'Here you go!'

The bartender then asks, 'Why are you so happy?'

And the guy says, 'Well, do you see that guy at the other end of the bar? I bet him $1000 that I could pee on you and you would be happy!'

PMS

Did you hear why the Army sent so many women with PMS to the Gulf War? Because they fought like animals and held water for four days.

There's a new all-female delivery service called PMS. They deliver when they fucking feel like it.

What's the difference between a woman with PMS and a pitbull terrier? Lipstick.

Why does it take five women with PMS to change a light bulb?
IT JUST DOES, ALL RIGHT!

PMS TEST

1 Everyone around you has an attitude problem.

2 You're adding chocolate chips to your cheese omelet.

3 The drier has shrunk every last pair of your jeans.

4 Your husband is suddenly agreeing to everything you say.

5 You're using your mobile phone to dial up every bumper sticker that says, 'How's my driving — call *** ****.'

6 Everyone's head looks like an invitation to batting practice.

7 You're convinced there's a God and he's male.

8 You're counting down the days until menopause.

9 You're sure that everyone is scheming to drive you crazy.

10 The valium bottle is empty and you bought it yesterday.

POETS

Poets William Shakespeare and Robbie Burns are both outside the pearly gates. St Peter scratches his head and says, 'Well, we only have room for one poet in Heaven, so we will have a contest! Whoever can write the better poem, gets in! The topic will be Timbuctoo.'

After an hour, the two poets come back to St Peter. Shakespeare goes first:

>'As I walk across the golden sands,
>A great big ship comes into view,
>Its destination Timbuctoo.'

St Peter says, 'OK, now we will hear Burns's poem.'

Burns says:

>'As Tim and I a-walking went,
>We saw three damsels by a tent,
>As they were three and we were two,
>I bucked one and Tim bucked two!'

POLICE BALLS

Police officers George and Mary had been assigned to walk the beat. They had only been out a short while when Mary said, 'Damn, I was running late this morning and when I was changing into my uniform I forgot to put on my panties! We have to go back to the station to get them.'

George replied, 'We don't have to go back. Just give Fido, my trusty police dog, one sniff and he will go fetch them for you.'

It was a hot day and Mary didn't fell like heading back to the station, so she lifted her skirt for the dog. Fido's nose shot between her legs, sniffing and snorting. After 10 seconds of sniffing, Fido's ears picked up, he sniffed the wind, and he was off in a flash towards the station house.

Five minutes went by and no sign of Fido. Ten minutes passed, and the dog was nowhere to be seen. Fifteen minutes passed, and they were starting to worry.

Twenty minutes passed, and they heard sirens in the distance. The sirens got louder and louder. Suddenly there, followed by a dozen police cars, was Fido rounding the corner — with the Desk Sergeant's balls in his mouth!

POLICEMAN

A motorcycle policeman had just pulled over a red Porsche after it had run a stop sign. 'May I see your driver's licence and registration, please.'

'What's the problem officer?'

'You just ran that stop sign back there.'

'Oh come on pal. There wasn't a car within cooee of me.'

'Nevertheless, sir, you are required to come to a complete stop, look both ways, and proceed with caution.'

'You must be kidding!'

'It's no joke, sir.'

'Look, I slowed down almost to a complete stop, saw no one within twenty kilometres, and proceeded with caution.'

'That's beside the point, sir. You are supposed come to a complete stop, and you didn't. Now, if I may see your licence and registration?'

'You've got a lot of time on your hands, mate. What's the matter, all the betting shops closed?'

'Sir, I'll overlook that last comment. Let me see your license and registration immediately.'

'I will if you can tell me the difference between slowing down and coming to a complete stop.'

The policeman had had enough. 'Sir, I can do better than that.' He opened the car door, dragged the rude motorist out, and proceeded to methodically beat him rapidly over the head.

'Now sir, would you like for me to slow down, or come to a complete stop?'

POLICE — HOW TO PISS THEM OFF

When you get pulled over, say, 'What's wrong, ossifer, there's no blood in my alcohol?'

When he asks why you were speeding, tell him you wanted to race.

When he talks to you, pretend you are deaf.

If he asks if you knew how fast you were going, say, 'No, my speedometer only goes to …'

Ask if you can see his gun. When he says you aren't allowed, tell him, 'I just wanted to see if mine was bigger.'

Ask him where he bought his cool hat.

If he asks you to step out of the car, throw yourself on the hood.

When he asks you to spread them, tell him you don't go that way.

When he puts the handcuffs on, say, 'Usually my dates buy me dinner first.'

Before you sign the ticket, pick your nose. Then ask to use his pen to sign the ticket. Chew on the pen, nervously. Clean your ear with the pen.

Ask him if he ever worked in a prison. If he says yes, ask him how the plumbing was.

When he comes to the car, say, 'I have a badge just like yours!'

When he frisks you, say, 'You missed a spot,' and grin.

When he asks to inspect your car, say, 'There is no alcohol in my car, sir, the last cop got it.'

Try to sell him your car. Ask if you can buy his car.

If he takes you to the station, ask to sit in front.

If you are female, say, 'I don't do that on the first date.'

Stare at his lights and say, 'Look at the pretty colours!'

Tell him you like men in uniform.

Ask if you can borrow his uniform for a fancydress party.

A police officer came upon a terrible car wreck where the driver and passenger had been killed. As he looked upon the wreckage a little monkey came out of the bush and hopped around the crashed car. The officer looked down at the monkey and said, 'I wish you could talk.' The monkey looked up at the officer and nodded his head up and down.
　'You can understand what I'm saying?' asked the officer. Again, the monkey nodded up and down.
　'Well, did you see this?'
　'Yes,' motioned the monkey.
　'What happened?' The monkey pretended to have a can in his hand and turned it up by his mouth.
　'They were drinking?' asked the officer.
　'Yes,' nodded the Monkey.
　'What else?' asked the officer. The monkey pinched his fingers together and held them to his mouth, sucking in quickly.
　'They were smoking marijuana too?' said the officer. 'Yes,' nodded the Monkey.

'What else?' queried the officer.

The monkey made a sexual sign with his fingers.

'So they were playing around too!?' asked the astounded officer.

'Yes,' nodded the monkey.

'Now wait, you're saying your owners were drinking, smoking and playing around before they wrecked the car?'

'Yes,' the Monkey nodded.

'What were you doing during all this?' asked the Officer.

'Driving,' motioned the monkey.

A police officer, though scheduled for all-night duty at the station, was relieved early and arrived home four hours ahead of schedule, at two in the morning. Not wanting to wake his wife, he undressed in the dark, crept into the bedroom and started to climb into bed. Just then, his wife sleepily sat up and said, 'Mike, dearest, would you go down to the all-night chemist and get me some aspirin? I've got a splitting headache.'

'Certainly, dear,' he said, and feeling his way across the dark room, he got dressed and walked over to the chemist.

As he arrived, the chemist looked up in surprise, 'G'day,' he said. 'I know you — you're a policeman, aren't you? Officer Fenwick, right?'

'Yeah, so?' said the officer.

'Well, what are you doing all dressed up like a fireman?'

POLICE TRANSLATOR
(WHAT IS SAID AND WHAT IS MEANT)

While on routine patrol ...
I was in the car because the coffee shop was closed.

The motorist was operating his vehicle in a reckless manner ...
He had a bumper sticker that said 'SLOW DOWN — DON'T FEED THE PIGS'

The accident scene and the safety of the victims prevented this officer from doing traffic control.
It was raining.

This officer went out-of-service to obtain intelligence information from a street informant.
It was too hot to ride in the car

I observed the suspect acting in a suspicious manner ...
The man let out an 'oink' as I walked by.

The members of the press at the scene were offered every courtesy within departmental policies...

I sent them to a non-existent address which I called the 'Command Post'.

I gave the motorist a verbal warning for speeding ... She was a good-looking blonde who owned a liquor store and who was free after my shift was over.

Further interview of the witnesses was impossible, due to conditions.
Tonight is my footy night ...

Using only enough force to restrain the subject ...

POLITICIANS

Five Collins Street surgeons are discussing who makes the best patients to operate on. The first surgeon says, 'I like to see accountants on my operating table, because when you open them up, everything inside is numbered.'

The second responds, 'Yeah, but you should try electricians! Everything inside them is colour coded.'

The third surgeon says, 'No, I really think librarians are the best; everything inside them is in alphabetical order.'

The fourth surgeon chimes in: 'You know, I like

construction workers ... those guys always understand when you have a few parts left over at the end, and when the job takes longer than you said it would.'

But the fifth surgeon shut them all up when he observed: 'You're all wrong. Politicians are the easiest to operate on. There's no guts, no heart, and no spine, and the head and arse are interchangeable.'

How can you tell when a politician is lying?
His lips are moving!

POMMIE BASTARDS

A young boy from Brunswick comes home from school and declares to his mother. 'I got initiated as an Australian today. I ate a pie and drank a can of beer.'

His Pommie mother said, 'Go straight to your bedroom your father will deal with you.'

Father comes home. Mother tells him her son has been drinking. Father goes into bedroom and belts the living daylights out of the boy.

Half an hour later the boy comes out still sobbing and declares, 'I've only been an true blue Aussie for less than three hours but already I hate you Pommie bastards!'

POOFTERS

Why do gay men wear ribbed condoms?
For traction in the mud.

Hear about the two queer ghosts?
They were running around putting the willies up each other.

What do you call a gay dinosaur?
Mega-sor-arse.

'Mum, I have something to tell you — I'm gay.'

'You're gay, doesn't that mean that men put their penises into your anus?'

'Yes mum, they do.'

'And you put other men's penises in your mouth?'

The faggot said nervously, 'Uh, yeah, Mum, I do.'

His mother went back to stirring the pot, then suddenly whirled around, and whacked him over the head with a frypan and said, 'Don't you dare complain about my cooking ever again!'

On a plane where a man was served by an obviously gay male flight attendant. The attendant announced 'The Captain has asked me to you all that he will be landing the big scary plane shortly, so if you could just put up your trays, that would be great.'

The man did as he had instructed but the woman next to him ignored him. A few moments later, the flight attendant came back and said to her, 'Ma'am, perhaps you couldn't hear me over the big scary engine, but I asked you to please put up your tray so that the captain can land the plane.'

She still wouldn't comply. Now he was getting angry and asked her again to put up the tray. She then calmly turned to him and said: 'In my country, I am called a princess. I take orders from no one.'

The flight attendant replied: 'Oh yeah? Well in MY country, I'm called a queen and I outrank you, bitch, so put the tray up!'

POPE

A man went to the Vatican, and waited in line for a long time. At last the pope emerged and proceeded down the line. The businessman was wearing his finest suit and was hoping that the pope would notice him.

To his disappointment, however, the pope went straight past him without so much as a glance, but stopped in front of a decrepit local tramp, leant forward and said a few words in the tramp's ear.

Afterwards the man went up to the tramp, and offered to trade his suit for the tramp's shabby outfit. The tramp readily agreed.

The next day the businessman went back to the Vatican wearing the tramp's gear, and to all appearances looking (and smelling) like a homeless bum. He waited in the line again until the pope emerged and proceeded down the line.

This time the pope noticed him immediately, came straight towards him, leant forward and whispered in his ear:

'I thought I told you yesterday to fuck off.'

The pope was failing fast and medical experts were called in from all over the world. They argued over the best approach to the crisis. At last they reached a consensus that a lifetime of celibacy had built up a huge store of seminal fluid that was choking the papal arteries. The only cure: an urgent course of intercourse.

The pope crossed himself and shook his head.

But the physicians were convincing. 'Your holiness, if you persist in celibacy, you'll condemn yourself to a speedy death. That is suicide, a mortal sin.'

The pope said he would pray for three days and consider the theological implications. On the third day he called the doctors to his bedside.

'I have come to a decision. I will be guided by your advice. But make sure she has big tits and gives a great blowjob.'

PORNO FLICK

Mike is hired to play his trumpet on the score of a movie, and he's excited. After the sessions, he asks the producer where and when he can catch the film. The producer explains that the music is for a porno flick that will be out in a month, and he tells Mike where he can go to see it.

A month later, Mike, with his collar up and wearing glasses, goes to the theatre. He sits way in the back, next to an elderly couple who also seem to be disguised and hiding.

The movie starts, and it's the filthiest, most perverse porno flick ever. Halfway through, a dog gets in on the action. Before anyone can blink an eye, the dog has had sex with all the women and most of the men.

Embarrassed, Mike turns to the old couple and whispers, 'I'm only here for the music.'

The woman turns to Mike and whispers back, 'We're only here to see our dog!'

PORSCHE & PORCUPINE

What is the difference between a Porsche and a porcupine?
The porcupine has pricks on the outside.

PORTRAIT

An elderly woman decided to have her portrait painted. She told the artist, 'Paint me with diamond earrings, a diamond necklace, emerald bracelets, a ruby broach, and gold Rolex.'

'But you are not wearing any of those things.'

'I know,' she said. 'It's in case I should die before my husband. I'm sure he will remarry right away, and I want his new wife to go crazy looking for the jewelry.'

POSITION?

Husband: Shall we try a different position tonight?
Wife: That's a good idea. You stand by the ironing board, while I sit on the sofa and fart.

POVERTY

We were so poor when I was growing up, we couldn't afford a roof to our mouths!

PREGNANT

There are two things in the air
that can make a woman pregnant.
Her legs.

PREPARING FOR A MAMMOGRAM

Many women are afraid of their first mammogram, but there is no need to worry. Do the following practice exercises, and you will be totally prepared.

EXERCISE #1
Freeze two metal bookends overnight.
Strip to the waist.
Invite a stranger into the room.
Press the bookends against one of your breasts.
Smash the bookends together as hard as you can.
Set an appointment with the stranger to meet next year and do it again.

EXERCISE #2
Open your refrigerator door and insert one breast between the door and the main box.
Have one of your strongest friends slam the door shut as hard as possible and lean on the door for good measure.
Hold that position for five seconds.
Repeat again in case the first time wasn't effective enough.

EXERCISE #3
Visit your garage at 3:00 a.m. when the temperature of the concrete floor is just perfect.
Take off all your warm clothes and lie comfortably on the floor with one breast wedged under the rear tire of the car.
Ask a friend to slowly back the car up until the breast is sufficiently flattened and chilled.
Turn over and repeat for the other breast.

PRIESTS

Two priests die at the same time and meet St Peter at the pearly pates. St Peter says, 'I'd like to get you in now, but our computer's down. You'll have to go back to earth for about a week, but you can't go back as humans. What'll it be?'

The first priest says, 'I've always wanted to be an eagle, soaring above the Ayers Rock. I really can do that?'

'So be it,' says St Peter, and off flies the first priest.

The second priest thinks for a moment and asks, 'Will any of this week count, St Peter?'

'No, I told you the computer's down. There's no way we can keep track of what you're doing. The week's a freebie.'

'In that case,' says the second priest, 'I've always wanted to be a stud.'

'So be it,' says St Peter, and the second priest disappears.

A week goes by, the computer is fixed, and God tells St Peter to recall the two priests. 'Will you have any trouble finding them?' He asks.

'The first one should be easy,' says St Peter. 'He's somewhere over Ayers Rock, flying with the eagles. But the second one could prove to be more difficult.'

'Why?' asked God.

St Peter answered, 'He's on a snow tyre somewhere in the Kosciousko National Park.'

What do a Christmas tree and a priest have in common?
Their balls are just for decoration.

PRIME MINISTERS

'By 1990, no Australian child
will be living in poverty.'
— Robert J. 'Bob' Hawke

'If you were my husband I'd poison you.'
                    (women interjector)
'Madam, if you were my wife, I'd take it.'
                    — Robert G. 'Bob' Menzies
          (this same quote has also been attributed to
                    Winston Churchill to Lady Astor)

PROFESSIONAL

A man met a beautiful lady and he decided he wanted to marry her right away. She said, 'But we don't know anything about each other.' He said, 'That's all right, we'll learn about each other as we go along.'

So she consented, and they were married, and went on a honeymoon to a very nice resort. One morning they were lying by the pool, when he got up off of his towel, climbed up to the 10-metre board and did a two and a half tuck gainer followed by a three rotations in jackknife position, where he straightened out and cut the water like a knife.

After a few more demonstrations, he came back and lay down on the towel. She said, 'That was incredible!'

He said, 'I used to be an Olympic diving champion. You see, I told you we'd learn more about ourselves as we went along.'

So she got up, jumped in the pool, and started doing laps. After about thirty laps she climbed back out and lay down on her towel hardly out of breath.

He said, 'That was incredible! You must have been

an Olympic endurance swimming champion?'

'No,' she said, 'I was a hooker in Venice and I worked both sides of the canal.'

PROSTITUTE

What do you call a Serbian prostitute?
Slobberdown Mycockyoubitch.

PUSSY

How do you know God meant men to eat pussies?
Why else would he make it look like a taco?

How does a man know when he's eaten pussy well?
When his face looks like a glazed doughnut.

Why is a pussy like a warm toilet seat?
Because they both feel good, but you wonder who was there before you.

How does a woman know when her pussy smells?
When a fly lands on it, throws up and dies.

What do you call that useless piece of skin around a pussy?
A woman.

What is the difference between a pussy and a cunt?
A pussy is warm and moist. A cunt is what owns it.

Q

QUEENSLANDERS

There were two Queenslanders wanting to pull down mangoes. They started to throw stones at the mangoes but it was impossible to hit one. One man told the other, 'How do we know if the mangoes we are trying to knock down are ripe and juicy.'

So the other one said, 'Why don't you go up the tree and see if the mangoes are ripe and juicy? That way we will know if we are just wasting time throwing stones at those mangoes.'

The first man came down and said, 'Yes, the mangoes are ripe and juicy. That means that we should keep on throwing stones until we hit them down..

QUESTION & ANSWER

What do you do if your woman starts smoking?
Slow down and use a lubricant.

What is the difference between erotic and kinky?
Erotic is using a feather; kinky is using the whole chicken.

What is the difference between 'ooooooh' and 'aaaaaaah'?
About three inches.

What is the difference between a hormone and an enzyme?
You can't hear an enzyme.

How many men does it take to screw in a light bulb?
One. Men will screw anything.

QUIZ FOR MEN
WHERE 'C' IS THE RIGHT ANSWER

1 You should make love to a woman for the first time only after you've both shared:
   a) Your views about what you expect from a sexual relationship
   b) Your blood-test results
   c) Five tequila slammers

2 You time your orgasm so that:
   a) Your partner climaxes first
   b) You both climax simultaneously
   c) You don't miss Sports Sunday

3 Passionate, spontaneous sex on the kitchen floor is:
   a) Healthy, creative love-play
   b) Not the sort of thing your wife/girlfriend would ever agree to doing
   c) Not the sort of thing your wife/girlfriend need ever find out about

4 Spending the whole night cuddling a woman you've just had sex with is:
   a) The best part of the experience
   b) The second best part of the experience
   c) $100 extra

5 Your girlfriend says she's gained two kilos in weight in the last month. You tell her that it is:

a) No concern of yours
   b) Not a problem—she can join your gym
   c) A conservative estimate

6 You think today's sensitive, caring man is:
   a) A myth
   b) An oxymoron
   c) A moron

7 Foreplay is to sex as:
   a) Appetiser is to entree
   b) Priming is to painting
   c) A queue is to an fairground ride

8 Which of the following are you most likely to find yourself saying at the end of a relationship?
   a) 'I hope we can still be friends.'
   b) 'I'm not in right now. Please leave a message after the tone ...'
   c) 'Welcome to Dumpsville. Population: You.'

9 A woman who is uncomfortable watching you masturbate:
   a) Probably needs a little more time before she can cope with that sort of intimacy
   b) Is uptight and a waste of time
   c) Shouldn't have sat next to you on the bus in the first place

R

REAL ESTATE AGENT LANGUAGE

A renovator's delight
(A rundown heap of shit that we hope some sucker will buy.)

Wonderful views
(Stand on the roof with a pair of binoculars and you can see the ocean.)

Quiet neighbourhood
(Nextdoor neighbour's kid only throws rocks at weekends.)

Tree-lined street
(Council planted 50 eucalypts but there's only two left unvandalised.)

Suit large family
(A big mother fucker of a house in need of total renovation.)

Near transport
(If you run like fuck every morning you might catch the twice daily bus.)

Close to school
(On the other side of that big brick wall that acts as a fence between you and three hundred little morons for most of the year.)

Street parking permit
(If you can find a spot not taken by some mothers who sit yacking to other mothers whilst waiting for school to break up for the day.)

Off-street parking
(If you can convince the bastard who parks his Toyota delivery van not to park in the laneway access to your property.)

Near the shops
(There a greasy fish and chip joint half a km down one end of the road, and a TAB at the other end.)

All amenities
The water pisses out everywhere when you go to the dunny.)

Birds naturally occur in garden
(Pigeons shit from your TV antennae, whilst sparrows crap on your washing.)

Native wildlife abounds
(There's a bloody possum in your ceiling chewing through your electrical wiring. There's a cat fight beneath your bedroom window at 3 a.m. each night when Tom shags the neighbour's Persian.)

Security
(The garage door lock is stuffed and no one can open it.)

Fresh air ventilation
(The window in the bathroom was smashed by a pervert trying to see any female in the shower.)

Water sprinkler system
(Some bastard ran over the hose with the Victa mower and water sprays in every direction.)

No Junk Mail
(The previous owner smashed the face in of an old lady delivering brochures to add a bit to her pension, now no one is game to enter the street.)

Quiet cul-de-sac
(A dark and lonely dead-end, that you wouldn't go down at night, for fear of your life.)

Chance of a lifetime
(If we don't offload this property to someone, we'll be stuck with it.)

Owner says sell!
(Yeah, he knows the house is fucked and will take anything just to get out.)

Heritage building at its best
(The place was built in 1843, and there's nothing but old shingles, paper plaster, white ants, rising damp, mildew, and a smell of decayed bodies in the cellar full of water.)

REJECTED GREETING CARDS

So your daughter's a hooker,
And it spoiled your day ...
Look at the bright side,
She's a really good lay!

My tyre was thumping,
I thought it was flat.
When I looked at the tyre,
I noticed your cat ... Sorry!

You had your bladder removed
And you're on the mends,
Here's a bouquet of flowers
And a box of ...

Happy vasectomy!
Hope you feel zippy!
'Cause when I had mine
I got real snippy!

Heard your wife left you,
How upset you must be.
But don't fret about it,
She moved in with me!

RESTAURANT

A man and a beautiful woman were having dinner in a fine restaurant. The waitress, taking an order at another table a few paces away, couldn't help but notice the man slowly sliding down his chair and under the table, yet the woman dining across from him appeared unconcerned.

The waitress continued to watch as the man slid all the way down his chair and out of sight under the table. Still, the woman dining across from him appeared calm and unruffled, apparently unaware that her dining companion had disappeared.

Once the waitress had finished taking the order, she walked over to the table and said to the woman, 'Pardon me, ma'am, but I think your husband just slid under the table.'

The woman calmly looked up at her and replied firmly, 'No, he didn't. My husband just walked into the restaurant.'

REVENGE

A bloke was really pissed off when he was dumped by his girlfriend and was desperate to win her back, even after he heard she had a new boyfriend. He tried everything, ringing, writing, sending flowers and still she wouldn't budge.

She was so fed up with his pestering that she decided she'd get rid of his attentions, so she sent him a photo of herself sucking a bloke's dick, with a note. 'Having a great time now that you're not here.'

The bloke was heartbroken, but angry, so posted the photo on to her parents with a note: 'Dear Mum and Dad, having a great time holidaying on the Gold Coast, wish you were here!'

RIBBONS

A woman goes to a vet and learns that that if you put a ribbon around a snoring dog's penis he'll roll over and stop snoring. The next night her dog is snoring so she goes to the kitchen, gets a red ribbon and ties it around her dog's dick. His snoring stops.

Later on that night her husband is snoring and so she goes to the kitchen, gets a blue ribbon and ties it around her husband's dick. He stops snoring.

Next morning her husband wakes up and looks at his dog and looks down at himself and says to his dog, 'I don't know what happened last night, but we came in first and second.'

ROAD TO GUNDAGAI

There's a T-model Ford
Made of wood and bits of board
Along the road to Gundagai.
The spark plugs are missing,

The radiator's hissing,
Along the road to Gundagai.
There's water in the petrol,
And there's sand in the gears
And it hasn't seen a garage
In more than forty years,
We're the boys,
We're the red hot saveloys,
We're on a track winding back
To our good old rooting shack
Along the road to Gundagai.

ROAD WORKER

At last Gerald got a job, working as a road worker for the Brisbane City Council. Day one at the depot and the men are getting their job allocations for the day. Each man is given a list of jobs and a tool.

When Gerald's turn comes and he is given his duties, he looks disappointed.

The foreman asks, 'What's wrong mate?'

'How come I don't get a shovel to lean on, too?'

ROOTER ROOSTER

A salesman is talking to a farmer when he looks over and sees a rooster wearing pants, a shirt, and suspenders. He says, 'What on earth is that all about?'

The farmer says, 'We had a fire in the chicken coop two months ago and all his feathers got singed off, so the wife made him some clothes to keep him warm.'

'OK, but that was two months ago. Why does he still wear them?'

The farmer replied, 'There ain't nothing funnier than watching him try to hold down a hen with one foot and get his pants down with the other.'

RULES THAT MEN WISH WOMEN KNEW

If you think you're fat, you probably are. Don't ask us.
Learn to work the toilet seat: If it's up, put it down.

Boys' haircuts are for boys, and you are not a boy.
Birthdays and anniversaries are not quests to see if he can find the perfect present, again.
If you ask a question you don't want an answer to, expect an answer you don't want to hear.

Sometimes he's not thinking about you. Live with it. Don't ask him what he's thinking about unless you are prepared to discuss such topics as cars, football, or sex.

Get rid of your cat. And no, its not different, it's just like every other cat. Dogs are better than ANY cats.

Sunday sports. It's like the full moon or the changing of the tides. Let it be.

Shopping is not sport.

Anything you wear is fine. Really.

You have enough clothes.

You have too many shoes.

Crying is blackmail. Use it if you must, but don't expect us to like it.

Your brother is an idiot, your ex-boyfriend is an idiot and your father probably is too.

Ask for what you want. Subtle hints don't work.

No, he doesn't know what day it is. He never will. Mark anniversaries on the calendar.

Yes, pissing standing up is more difficult than peeing from point blank range. We're bound to miss sometimes.

Most men own two or three pairs of shoes. What makes you think that we would be any good at choosing which pair, out of thirty, would look good with your dress.

Yes and no are perfectly acceptable answers.

A headache that lasts for 17 months is a problem. See a doctor.

Your mother doesn't HAVE to be your best friend.

Foreign films are best left to foreigners.

Check your oil.

Don't give us 50 rules when 25 will do.

Don't fake it. We'd rather be ineffective than deceived.

It is neither in your best interests or ours to take a magazine quiz together.

Anything we said 6 or 8 months ago is inadmissible in an argument.

All comments become null and void after seven days.

If something we said could be interpreted two ways and one of the ways makes you sad or angry, we meant the other way.

Let us ogle. If we don't look at other women, how can we appreciate how pretty you are.

Don't rub the lamp if you don't want the genie to come out.

You can either ask us to do something OR tell us how you want it done — not both.

Whenever possible, please say whatever you have to say during commercials.

Captain Cook didn't need directions, and neither do we.

Women wearing wonderbras and low-cut blouses lose their right to complain about having their boobs stared at.

Consider sport playing as a mini-vacation from you. We need it, you need it.

Telling us that the models in the men's magazine are airbrushed makes you look jealous and petty and it's certainly not going to deter us from reading the magazines.

The relationship is never going to be like it was the first two months we were going out.

S

SANDWICHES

Two lawyers go into a restaurant and ordered two drinks. Then they produced sandwiches from their briefcases and started to eat.

The owner became quite worried and marched

over and told them, 'You can't eat your own sandwiches in here!'

The lawyers looked at each other, shrugged their shoulders and then exchanged sandwiches.

SCAM

Australian police have been unable to recommend a prosecution for the following scam: A company takes out a newspaper advertisement claiming to be able to supply imported hard-core pornographic videos. As their prices seem reasonable, people place orders and make payments via cheque.

After several weeks the company writes back explaining that under the present law they are unable to supply the materials and do not wish to be prosecuted. So they return their customers money in the form of a company cheque. However, due to the name of the company, few people ever bother to present these to their banks.

The name of the company is 'The Anal Sex and Fetish Perversion Company'.

SCHOOL

Early one morning, a mother went in to wake up her son. 'Wake up, son. It's time to go to school!'

'But why, Mum? I don't want to go.'

'Give me two reasons why you don't want to go.'

'Well, the kids hate me for one, and the teachers hate me, too!'

'Oh, that's no reason not to go to school. Come on now and get ready.'

'Give me two reasons why I should go to school.'

'Well, for one, you're 52 years old. And for another, you're the teacher!'

A mother is having an argument with her young son who is screaming he doesn't want to go back school after holidays. His mother tries to take the upper hand. 'Look Brian, I'm sorry but I don't think that you're school is undergoing cutbacks and that you've been laid off!

SCOTCH

A man stopped at his favourite watering hole after a hard day's work to relax. He noticed a man next to him ordered a shot and a beer. The man drank the shot, chased it with the beer and then looked into his shirt pocket.

He did this several times as the first man watched. The first man's curiosity got the better of him. He leaned over and said, 'Excuse me, I couldn't help notice your little ritual. Why in the world do you look into your shirt pocket every time you drink your shot and beer?'

The man replied, 'There's a photo of my wife in there, and when she starts to look good then I know it's time to go home.'

SCREAM

How do you get your wife to scream for hours after sex?
Wipe your dick on the curtains.

How do you make a woman scream twice?
Screw her up the arse, then wipe your dick on the curtains.

SEAMAN

A seaman meets a pirate in a bar, and they take turns to tell their adventures on the seas. The seaman notes that the pirate has a peg-leg, hook, and an eye patch.

The seaman asks 'So, how did you end up with the peg-leg?'

The pirate replies, 'We were in a storm at sea, and I was swept overboard into a school of sharks. Just as my men were pulling me out, a shark bit my leg off.'

'Wow!' said the seaman. 'What about the hook?'

'Well ...' replied the pirate, 'We were boarding an enemy ship and were battling the other sailors with swords. One of the enemy cut my hand off.'

'Incredible!' remarked the seaman. 'How did you get the eye patch?'

'A seagull dropping fell into my eye,' replied the pirate.

'You lost your eye to a seagull dropping?' the sailor asked incredulously.

'Well ...' said the pirate, '... it was my first day with the hook.'

SEX

Remember if you smoke after sex you are doing it too fast.

A man and his wife are having sex. Fifteen minutes has passed, 30 minutes, then 45 minutes. Sweat is pouring off both of them. The wife finally looks up and says, 'What's the matter, darling, can't you think of anyone else, either?'

Love is the answer
but while you're waiting,
sex raises some pretty good questions.
—Woody Allen, actor/director

I never miss a chance to have sex or appear on television.
— Gore Vidal, US writer

Sex without love is a meaningless experience,
But as a meaningless experience sex is pretty damn good.
— Woody Allen

SEX ADVICE FROM MEN FOR INNOCENT WOMEN

Q: How do I know if I'm ready for sex?
A: Ask your boyfriend. He'll know when the time is right. When it comes to love and sex, men are much more responsible, since they're not emotionally confused as women.

Q: Should I have sex on the first date?
A: YES. Before if possible.

Q: What exactly happens during the act of sex?
A: Again, this is entirely up to the man. The important thing to remember is that you must do whatever he tells you without question. Sometimes he may ask you to do certain things that may at first seem strange to you. Do them anyway.

Q: How long should the sex act last?
A: This is a natural and normal part of nature, so don't feel ashamed or embarrassed. After you've finished making love, he'll have a natural desire to leave you suddenly, and go out with his friends to play golf or going out with his friends to the bar for the purpose of consuming large amounts of alcohol and sharing a few personal thoughts with his buddies. Don't feel left out — while he's gone you can busy yourself by doing laundry, cleaning the apartment, or perhaps even going out to buy him an expensive gift. He'll come back when he's ready.

Q: What is 'afterplay'?
A: After a man has finished making love, he needs

to replenish his manly energy. 'Afterplay' is simply a list of important activities for you to do after lovemaking. This includes lighting his cigarette, making him a sandwich or pizza, bringing him a few beers, or leaving him alone to sleep while you go out and buy him an expensive gift.

Q: Does the size of the penis matter?
A: Yes. Although many women believe that quality, not quantity, is important, studies show this is simply not true. The average erect male penis measures about 3 inches. Anything longer than that is extremely rare and, if by some chance your lover's sexual organ is 4 inches or over, you should go down on your knees and thank your lucky stars and do everything possible to please him, such as doing his laundry, cleaning his flat and/or buying him an expensive gift.

What about the female orgasm?
What about it?

How can you tell if a man is sexually excited?
He's breathing.

SEX DOGGIE STYLE

Des: My wife is into dingo sex.
Dave: Dingo sex?
Des: Yeah, she makes me sit outside the hole, and howl all night!

Waiting for their morning bus two men noticed two dogs having sex in someone's front lawn.

'Look,' he shouted, 'What are the those dogs doing? Fighting?'

'They're having sex. Don't tell me that you have never had sex doggie style before.'

'Well no.'

'You have to try it. It's pretty cool. Here's what you do. Tonight when you get home, fix your wife a strong vodka and then suggest that you want to try this new sexual position.'

The man thought a bit, and said he would give it a try.

The next morning, the two commuters were waiting for the bus.

'Well, how did it go?'

His companion replied, 'It was great. But it took me SIX glasses of vodka just to get her naked in the front yard!'

Bill: My wife is into dog sex.
Ben: You mean she likes it doggie style?
Bill: No, she likes dog sex.
Ben: What, you mean bestiality?
Bill: No, I sit up and beg, and she rolls over and plays dead.

SHEILA

Australian colloq. Woman. Female of the species, (sometimes thought of as a species all on their own). Created by God as a mate for Adam. Created from Adams's seventh rib as an afterthought by God. Another of God's possible boo-boos.)

Woman, women (pl.), womyn (feminism), girl, lady, Ms, Miss, Missus, Mum, Mummy, Mother, Ma, Grandma, Gran, daughter, sister, sis, Aunt, Auntie.

trouble 'n' strife, old cheese, the old girl, spunk, sex magnet, doll, gorgeous, a bod, widgie, girlie, little lady, sex on legs, fuck, harlot, cunt, mole, scrubber, slash, tart, sausage root, rag, scrag, slut, bleeder, a BUR (beaut ute root), dick muncher, cock sucker, Hag, Shag, bitch, bike, Lesbian, lesbo, leso, dyke, muffdiver, muffmuncher, fannymuncher.

A ute without a dog is like shagging without a sheila — kinda lonesome.

Bruce is driving over the Sydney Harbour Bridge one day in his ute when he sees his girlfriend Sheila just about to throw herself off and into the water far below.

Bruce slams on the anchors and shouts, 'G'day

Sheila! What do you think your doing?'

Sheila turns around with a tear in her eye and says, 'G'day Bruce — you got me pregnant and so now I'm gonna kill myself.'

Bruce gets a lump in his throat when he hears this and says, 'Sheila, not only are you a great shag, but you're a real sport too!':

SHITTY FAN

A bloke has to take a crap really badly so he goes into a bar. He thinks the toilet is upstairs but he can't find it anywhere. He finds a hole in the floor so he takes a crap in it. After that he goes downstairs and there is no one down there so he asks the bartender were everyone is and he says, 'Where the hell were you when shit hit the fan?'

SHIT...

More lingo

You can be shit faced, be shit out of luck, or have shit for brains. With a little effort you can get your shit together, find a place for your shit or decide to shit or get off the pot. You can smoke shit, buy shit, sell shit, lose shit, find shit, forget shit and tell others to eat shit and die. You can shit or go blind, have a shit fit or just shit your life away.

People can be shit headed, shit brained, shit blinded, and shit over.

Some people know their shit while others can't tell the difference between shit and shineola.

There are lucky shits, dumb shits, crazy shits and sweet shits. There is bull shit, dog shit, cat shit, bird shit, whale shit, rat shit and horse shit. There is tough shit, hard shit, soft shit, slimy shit, rough shit, limp shit.

You can shit a blue streak, shit bricks, shit pink twinkies, shit marbles or shit your guts out.

You can throw shit, sling shit, catch shit or duck when the shit hits the fan. You can take a shit, give a shit, keep shit or serve shit on a shingle.

You can find yourself in deep shit or be happy as a pig in shit.

Some days are colder than shit, some hotter than shit and some days are just plain shitty.

There is funny shit and sad shit, bad shit and good shit.

Some shit doesn't stink while other things really smell like shit, some music sounds like shit, things can look like shit, and there are times when you feel like shit.

You can be faster than shit or you can be slower than shit.

Sometimes you'll find shit on a stick, sometimes you'll find shit everywhere, and then there are times when you can't find shit at all.

You can have too much shit, not enough shit, the right shit, the wrong shit or a lot of weird shit.

You can carry shit in a bucket, put shit in a barrel, have a pile of shit, have a mountain of shit, have a river of shit, or find yourself up shit creek without a paddle.

You can slice shit, spread shit, dunk shit or jump shit and some people just can't cut the shit.

There is fun shit and dull shit, silly shit and serious shit.

Sometimes you really need this shit and sometimes you don't want any shit at all. You can stir shit, kick shit or stick your arse out of the window and shit on the world. Sometimes everything you touch turns to shit and other times you swim in a lake of shit and come out smelling like a rose.

Shit! When you stop to consider all the facts, it's the basic building block of creation. This means the universe did not begin with a BIG BANG but with a BIG DUMP. Keep that in mind the next time you flush the toilet.

SHOWGIRL AND OLD CODGER

A flashy showgirl married a 97-year-old retired well-to-do businessman, largely because she held the belief that the old codger wouldn't even survive the wedding night.

While her new husband was in the bathroom, the woman slipped into a black see-through nightie and struck her most seductive pose on the bed. When the old man finally emerged, she was startled to see that he was stark naked except for earplugs, a clothes-pin on his nose and a condom.

'Why are you wearing those?' she asked in amazement.

'Because if there's anything I just can't stand,' he grumbled, 'It's the sound of a woman screaming and the smell of burning rubber.'

SICK

Sue was feeling pretty sick, so told her boss she was going home. Her boss had just got over the 'flu himself so was quite understanding. 'OK Sue, take care now. I hope it isn't something I gave you.'

With that she burst into tears and ran from the office.

Mystified, he looked at Sandra, 'What did I say?'

She smiled and said, 'She's unmarried and she's got morning sickness!'

SIGNS

In the front yard of a funeral home:
'Drive carefully, we'll wait.'

On an electrician's truck:
'Let us remove your shorts.'

Outside a radiator repair shop:
'Best place in town to take a leak.'

In a non-smoking area:
'If we see you smoking, we will assume you are on fire and take appropriate action.'

On maternity room door:
'Push, Push, Push.'

On a front door:
'Everyone on the premises is a vegetarian except the dog.

At an optometrist's office:
'If you don't see what you're looking for, you've come to the right place.'

On a taxidermist's window:
'We really know our stuff.'

On a butcher's window:
'Let me meat your needs.'

On a fence:
'Salesmen welcome. Dog food is expensive.'

At a car dealership:
'The best way to get back on your feet — miss a car payment.'

Outside a muffler shop:
'No appointment necessary. We'll hear you coming.'

In a dry cleaner's shop:
'Drop your pants here.'

On a desk in a reception room:
'We shoot every third salesman, and the second one just left.'

In a veterinarian's waiting room:
'Be back in 5 minutes. Sit! Stay!'

In a beauty shop:
'Dye now!'

On the side of a garbage truck:
'We've got what it takes to take what you've got.'

In a restaurant window:
'Don't stand there and be hungry, come in and get fed up.'

Inside a bowling alley:
'Please be quiet. We need to hear a pin drop.'

In a cafeteria:
'Shoes are required to eat in the cafeteria. Socks can eat anywhere they want.'

For Sale: Parachute. Only used once, never opened, small stain.

SINNER

There once was a young woman who went to confession. Upon entering the confessional she said, 'Forgive me, Father, for I have sinned.'

The priest replied, 'Confess your sins and be forgiven.'

'Last night, my boyfriend made passionate love to me seven times.'

The priest thought long and hard and then said, 'Take seven lemons, squeeze them into a glass, and then drink the juice.

'Will this cleanse me of my sins, Father?'
'No, but it will wipe that smile off of your face.'

SISSY

One summer evening, during a violent thunderstorm, a mother was tucking her small boy into bed. She was about to turn off the light when he asked with a tremor in his voice, 'Mummy, will you sleep with me tonight?'

The mother smiled and gave him a reassuring hug. 'I can't, dear,' she said, 'I have to sleep with Daddy.'

A long silence was broken at last by a shaken little voice saying, 'The big sissy.'

SIXTY-NINER

What is the bad thing about the 69 position?
The view.

SMART

What's the smartest thing that ever came out of a woman's mouth?
Albert Einstein's dick.

SMOKING

What should you do if your wife starts smoking?
Slow down and use a lubricant

SNAILS

A wife and her husband were having a dinner party for some important guests. The wife was very excited about this and wanted everything to be perfect. At the very last minute, she realised that she didn't have any snails for the dinner party, so she asked her husband to run down to the beach with the bucket to gather some snails. Very grudgingly he agreed. He took the bucket, walked out the door, down the steps, and on to the beach. As he was collecting the snails, he noticed a beautiful woman strolling alongside the water just a little further down the beach. He kept thinking to himself, 'Wouldn't it be great if she would just come down and talk to me?' He went back to gathering the snails. All of a sudden he looked up, and the beautiful woman was standing right next to him.

They started talking and she invited him back to her place. They ended up spending the night together. At seven o'clock the next morning he woke up and exclaimed, 'Oh no! My wife's dinner party!' He gathered all his clothes, dressed speedily, grabbed his bucket, and ran out the door. He ran down the beach all the way to his apartment. He ran up the stairs of his apartment.

He was in such a hurry that when he got to the top of the stairs, he dropped the bucket of snails. There were snails all down the stairs.

The door opened just then, with a very angry wife standing in the door way wondering where he'd been all this time. He looked at the snails all down the steps, then he looked at her, then back at the snails and said, 'Come on, guys, we're almost there!'

SNOOKER

A world champion snooker player had just got married. It was the first night of his honeymoon.

His beautiful wife lay spread across the bed wearing only a scanty black silk nightdress.

Presently he came out of the bathroom totally naked with a long stiff erection and walked slowly to the foot of the bed. He didn't utter a sound but simply stood there looking at her and chalking the end of his erect penis. This went on for over ten minutes, the only movement being the slow rhythmic chalking of the tip of his penis and the movement of his head from side to side as he stared at her lying on the bed.

Eventually, moist with excitement and shaking with anticipation, she tore off her night dress and slowly spread her legs wide open waiting for him to take her. He simply raised his eyebrows, cocked his head to the side and continued to slowly stroke the soft chalk across the glistening, throbbing penis as he stared intently at the pleasures he saw between her outspread legs. It was too much for her to stand, writhing in an agony of expectation and frustration she screamed out, 'For God's sake what are you waiting for?'

He gently stroked the chalk across his throbbing penis, blew the loose chalk off its end, smiled and, looking even more closely between her smooth thighs, quietly told her, 'I'm trying to decide whether to go for the tight brown or the easy pink.'

SOAP AND WATER

A minister was asked to dinner by one of his parishioners, who he knew was an unkempt housekeeper. When he sat down at the table, he noticed that the dishes were the dirtiest that he had ever seen in his life.

'Were these dishes ever washed?' he asked his hostess, running his fingers over the grit and grime.

She replied, 'They're as clean as soap and water could get them.'

He felt a bit apprehensive, but blessed the food anyway and started eating. It was really delicious and he said so, despite the dirty dishes.

When dinner was over, the hostess took the dishes outside and yelled to the dogs, 'Here Soap! Here Water!'

SOME THOUGHTS

If Barbie is so popular, why do you have to buy her friends?

Why do psychics have to ask you for your name?

I couldn't repair your brakes, so I made your horn louder.

I drive way too fast to worry about cholesterol.

Depression is merely anger without enthusiasm.

Drink 'til she's cute, but stop before the wedding.

Eagles may soar, but rabbits don't get sucked into jet engines.

Early bird gets the worm, but the second mouse gets the cheese.

I almost had a psychic girlfriend but she left me before we met.

I intend to live for ever — so far, so good.

Mental backup in progress — Do Not Disturb.

Support bacteria — they're the only culture some people have.

I'm not cheap, but I am on special this week.

The only substitute for good manners is fast reflexes.

When everything's coming your way, you're in the wrong lane.

Ambition is a poor excuse for not having enough sense to be lazy.

Beauty is in the eye of the beer holder ...

24 hours in a day ... 24 beers in a case ... coincidence?

If I worked as much as others, I would do as little as they.

Many people quit looking for work when they find a job.

When I'm not in my right mind, my left mind gets pretty crowded.

Everyone has a photographic memory. Some don't have film.

If you choke a Smurf, what colour does it turn?

What happens if you get scared half to death twice?

I used to have an open mind but my brains kept falling out.

Shin: a device for finding furniture in the dark.

How do you tell when you run out of invisible ink?

OK, we know the speed of light, but what's the speed of dark?

I tried sniffing Coke once, but the ice cubes got stuck in my nose.

SPERM

A student at a Melbourne university was taking a cell biology course. The task of the day was examining epitheleal cheek cells under a microscope. The students had to scrape the inside of their mouths with a toothpick and make a slide from it and record the different types of cells that were found.

One girl in the class was having some trouble identifying some cells. She called the professor over to ask him. After a moment or two of peering in her scope, he looked up and said in a loud voice,

'Those are sperm cells.'

A wino was sitting at a bar, quietly sobbing into his beer.

The bartender asked, 'What's the problem, mate?'

The wino said, 'I just found out that sperm banks pay $20 for a donation.'

'So,' asked the bartender, 'why are you crying?'

'I've let a fortune slip through my fingers!' the wino wailed.

STAGES OF LIFE (MALE)

AGE/DRINK
17 Beer
25 Bourbon
35 Vodka
48 Double vodka
66 Bonox

AGE/SEDUCTION LINE
17 My parents are away for the weekend.
25 My girlfriend is away for the weekend.
35 My fiancée is away for the weekend.
48 My wife is away for the weekend.
66 My second wife is dead.

AGE/FAVOURITE SPORT
17 Sex
25 Sex
35 Sex

48 Sex
66 Napping

AGE/DEFINITION OF A SUCCESSFUL DATE
17 'Tongue'
25 'Breakfast'
35 'She didn't set back my therapy.'
48 'I didn't have to meet her kids.'
66 'Got home alive.'

AGE/FAVOURITE FANTASY
17 Getting to third
25 Airplane sex
35 Ménage-à-trois
48 Taking the company public
66 Swiss maid/Nazi love slave

AGE/THE IDEAL AGE TO GET MARRIED?
17 Twenty-five
25 Thirty-five
35 Forty-eight
48 Sixty-six
66 Seventeen

AGE/IDEAL DATE
17 Triple Stephen King feature at a drive-in
25 'Split the check before we go back to my place'
35 'Just come over'
48 'Just come over and cook'
66 'Oral sex in company jet on the way to Gold Coast'

STAGES OF LIFE (FEMALE)

AGE/DRINK
17 Wine coolers
25 White wine
35 Red wine
48 Dom Perignon
66 Shot of Black Label with caviar

AGE/EXCUSES FOR REFUSING DATES
17 Need to wash my hair
25 Need to wash and condition my hair
35 Need to colour my hair
48 Need to have François colour my hair
66 Need to have François colour my wig

AGE/FAVOURITE SPORT
17 Shopping
25 Shopping
35 Shopping
48 Shopping
66 Shopping

AGE/DEFINITION OF A SUCCESSFUL DATE
17 Hungry Jacks
25 Free meal
35 A diamond
48 A bigger diamond
66 Home alone

AGE/FAVOURITE FANTASY
17   Tall, dark and handsome
25   Tall, dark and handsome with money
35   Tall, dark and handsome with money and a brain
48   A man with hair
66   Aman

AGE/THE IDEAL AGE TO GET MARRIED?
17   Seventeen
25   Twenty-five
35   Thirty-five
48   Forty-eight
66   Sixty-six

AGE/IDEAL DATE
17   He offers to pay.
25   He pays.
35   He cooks breakfast the next morning.
48   He cooks breakfast the next morning for the kids.
66   He can chew breakfast.

STOCKMEN

Three stockman are sitting around a campfire, out on the end of the desert country, each yarning with the bravado for which stockmen are famous. A night of tall tales begins.

The first says, 'I must be the meanest, toughest stockman there is. Why, just the other day, a bull got loose in the paddock and gored six men before I wrestled it to the ground, by the horns, with my bare hands.'

The second can't stand to be beaten. 'That's nothing. I was walking down the track yesterday and a six-foot black snake slid out from under a rock and made a move for me. I grabbed that snake with my bare hands, bit its head off, and sucked the poison down in one gulp. And I'm still here today.'

The third stockman remained silent, slowly stirring the coals with his penis.

STRAIGHT SHOOTER

'So let me get this straight,' the barrister says to the defendant, 'You came home from work early and found your wife in bed with a strange man.'

'That's correct,' says the defendant.

'Upon which,' continues the barrister, 'You took out a pistol and shot your wife, killing her.'

'That's correct,' says the defendant.

'Then my question to you is, why did you shoot your wife and not her lover?' asked the barrister.

'It seemed easier,' replied the defendant, 'than shooting a different man every day!'

SUCKER

What do you call a woman who can suck an orange through a hose?
Darling.

Your wife and job are different.
Your job still sucks after five years.

SYDNEY SCREW

A depressed young woman was so desperate that she decided to end her life by throwing herself into the ocean. When she went down to the wharf at Sydney docks, a handsome young sailor noticed her tears, took pity on her, and said, 'Look, you've got a lot to live for. I'm off to Europe in the morning, and if you like, I can stow you away on my ship. I'll take good care of you and bring you food every day.'

Moving closer, he slipped his arm around her shoulder and added, 'I'll keep you happy, and you'll keep me happy.'

The girl nodded, 'Yes.' After all, what did she have to lose? That night, the sailor brought her aboard and hid her in a lifeboat. From then on, every night he brought her three sandwiches and a piece of fruit, and they made passionate love until dawn.

Three weeks later, during a routine search, she was discovered by the captain. 'What are you doing here?' the captain asked.

'I have an arrangement with one of the sailors,' she explained. 'He's taking me to Europe, and he's screwing me.'

'He sure is, lady ... This is the Manly Ferry!'

T

TALK DIRTY

Q: What is it when a man talks dirty?
A: Sexual harassment.

Q: What is it when a woman talks dirty?
A: About $5.00 a minute.

TAMPONS

How can you tell when a women is macho?
She rolls her own tampons.

Why do women skydivers always wear tampons?
So they don't whistle on the way down.

Tampons?
Vampire's teabags.

TATTOOS

A guy walks into a tattoo shop and tells the tattoo artist that he needs to have a perfect $100 bill tattooed on his penis.

The artist says to him, 'That will be very painful!'
The man replies, 'I don't care.'
The artist then says, 'It will take a long time.'
'I don't care, I have all the time you need,' replies the man.
The tattoo artist states, 'It will cost you a lot of money.'
'Money is no object! I must have this done.'
So the artist agrees. Two weeks goes by and the job is complete. The man looks at his penis and says, 'It is perfect ... you have thought of everything, even the serial number is there.'
The tattoo artists says to the man, 'Usually I don't ask about tattoos, but I have to know why you

wanted that done to your penis?'

The man replies, 'Well, I like to play with my money ... I like to watch my money grow ... and the next time my wife decides to blow a hundred dollars, she can stay at home and do it!'

TAX

'The trick is to stop thinking of it as 'your' money'. (tax auditor)

'The hardest thing in the world to understand is income tax!' (Albert Einstein)

'When there is an income tax, the just man will pay more and the unjust less on the same amount of income.' (Plato)

'There are two distinct classes of men ... those who pay taxes and those who receive and live upon taxes.' (Thomas Paine)

'The government that robs Peter to pay Paul can always depend upon the support of Paul.' (George Bernard Shaw)

'He who has the base necessities of life should pay nothing; taxation on him who has a surplus may, if need be; extend to everything beyond necessities.' (Rousseau)

'Like mothers, taxes are often misunderstood, but seldom forgotten.' (Lord Bramwell)

'War involves in its progress such a train of unforeseen and unsupposed circumstances that no human wisdom can calculate the end. It has but one thing certain, and that is to increase taxes.' (Thomas Paine)

'In the matter of taxation, every privilege is an injustice.' (Voltaire)

'But in this world nothing is certain but death and taxes.' (Benjamin Franklin)

'A taxpayer is someone who works for the federal government but who doesn't have to take a civil service examination.' (Ronald Reagan)

'There can be no doubt concerning the duty of each citizen to bear a part of the public expense. But the state on its part, insofar as it is charged with protecting and promoting the common good of its citizens, is under an obligation to assess upon them only necessary levies, which are, furthermore, proportionate to their means.' (Pius XII)

TAXI!

A boy and his date were parked on a back road some distance from town. Things were getting hot and heavy when the girl stopped the boy.

'I really should have mentioned this earlier, but I'm actually a hooker and I charge $20 for sex,' she said.

He reluctantly paid her, and gave her the best root he could. Afterwards she gets back into the front seat to head home, but he just sits there.

'Why aren't we going anywhere?' asked the girl.

'Well, I should have mentioned this before, but I'm actually a taxi driver, and the fare back to town is $25.'

One dismal rainy night in Sydney, a taxi driver spotted an arm waving from the shadows of an alley halfway down the block. Even before he rolled to a stop at the curb, a figure leaped into the cab and slammed the door. Checking his rear-view mirror as he pulled away, he was startled to see a dripping wet, naked woman sitting in the back seat.

'Where to, Miss?' he stammered.

'Kings Cross,' answered the woman.

'You got it,' he said, taking another long glance in the mirror.

The woman caught him staring at her and asked, 'Just what the hell are you looking at driver?'

'Well, madam,' he answered, 'I was just wondering how you'll pay your fare?'

'The woman spread her legs, put her feet up on the front seat, smiled at the driver and said, 'Does this answer your question?'

Still looking in the mirror, the cabby asked, 'Got anything smaller?'

TAXIDERMIST

A Pommie taxidermist is making his way along the Tasmanian coast sightseeing, when he comes across a pub in the middle of nowhere. He goes in, pushes his way between the beer-swilling locals and in his well-educated voice asks the barman, 'May I have a gin and tonic, please, my good man?'

One of the locals says to his mates, 'Gees, what kind of a fucking man's drink is that? Then, turning to the Englishman, 'Hey you! Yes, you, you fucking pom! Gin and fucking tonic — are you some kind of a poofter or something?'

'Actually,' the Englishman, replies nervously, 'I'm a taxidermist.'

'Oh yeah! And what's a taxidermist then?'

'I mount d... d... dead animals.'

'It's all right,' says the local, turning to his mates,'He's one of us!'

TEENAGE SEX

It was a dark spot in the Adelaide hills, a well-known lovers' lane that the police car headed down. Only one car tonight and the policeman could see two people in the back seat.

'How old are you mate?' the police officer asks as he shines the torch into the back.

A young man who is reading a book says, 'I'm nineteen, officer.'

A young girl sits next to the youth and she is busy knitting.

The officer says, 'And how old is the young lady, then?'

The young man replies, 'Mate, in about ten minutes she'll be sixteen and old enough to forget about knitting!'

TESTS

Two young men were sitting outside a clinic. One of them was crying like anything.
Second man: 'Why are you crying?'
First man: 'I came here for a blood test.'
Second man: 'So? Why are you crying? Are you afraid?'
First man: 'No. Not that. For the blood test, they cut my finger.'
At this, the second one started crying. The first one was astonished.
First man: 'Why are you crying?'
Second man: 'I've come for a urine test!'

THEY SAY THOSE THINGS WILL KILL YOU...

There was a gentleman from Korea who was killed by his mobile phone. More or less. He was doing the usual 'walking and talking' when he walked into a tree and managed to break his neck.

Keep that in mind the next time you decide to drive and dial at the same time.

TITS

(ball busters, balloons, bazookers, boobs, bristols, dolly partons, funbags, home, honkers, hooters, jugs, knockers, mammaries, montezumas, norgs, titties)

Why do women have tits?
So men will talk to them.

A guy named John goes over to his friend's house, rings the bell, and the wife answers.

'Hi! Is Tony home?'

'No, he went to the store.'

'Well, you mind if I wait?'

'No, come in.'

They sit down and John says, 'You know Betsy, you have the greatest looking breasts I have ever seen. I'd give you a hundred dollars if I could just see one.'

Betsy thinks about this for a second and says to herself, what the hell — a hundred dollars! My husband sees it all the time for free! So she opens her dress and shows one. John promptly thanks her and throws a $100 note on the table.

They sit there a while longer and John says, 'They are so beautiful, I've got to see both of them. I'll give you another hundred dollars if I could just see both of them together.'

Betsy thinks about this again and says what the hell, opens her dress and gives John a nice long look. John thanks her and throws another hundred dollars on the table, then says he can't wait any longer for Tony and leaves.

A while later Tony arrives home and his wife says, 'You know, your weird friend John came over.'

Tony promptly asks, 'Well, did he drop off the two hundred dollars he owes me?'

TOP TEN THINGS
ONLY WOMEN UNDERSTAND

10. Cats' facial expressions
9. The need for the same style of shoes in different colours
8. Why bean sprouts aren't just weeds
7. Fat clothes
6. Taking a car trip without trying to beat your best time
5. The difference between beige, off-white, and eggshell
4. Cutting your bangs to make them grow
3. Eyelash curlers
2. The inaccuracy of every bathroom scale ever made

And the number one thing only women understand:

1. OTHER WOMEN

TRAINING COURSES
FOR MEN

1. Introduction to Common Household Objects I: The Mop
2. Introduction to Common Household Objects II: The Sponge
3. Dressing Up: Beyond the Funeral and the Wedding
4. Refrigerator Forensics: Identifying and Removing the Dead

5	Pattern or Stain on the Carpet?: You CAN Tell the Difference!
6	It's Empty, You Can Throw It Away: Accepting Loss I
7	If the Milk Expired Three Weeks Ago, Keeping It In the Refrigerator Won't Bring It Back: Accepting Loss II
8	The Supermarket: It's Not Just for Women
9	Recycling Skills I: Boxes that the Electronics Came In
10	Recycling Skills II: Styrofoam that Came in the Boxes that the Electronics Came In
11	Bathroom Etiquette I: How to Remove Beard Clippings from the Sink
12	Bathroom Etiquette II: Let's Wash Those Towels
13	Bathroom Etiquette III: Five Easy Ways to Tell When You're About to Run Out of Toilet Paper
14	Giving Back to the Community: How to Donate 15-Year-Old Levis to the Salvos!
15	Retro? Or Just Hideous?: Re-examining Your 1970s Polyester Shirts
16	No, The Dishes Won't Wash Themselves: Knowing the Limitations of Your Kitchenware
17	Romance: More Than a Cable Channel!
18	Strange But True!: She Really May NOT Care What 'Fourth Down and Ten' Means!
19	Going Out to Dinner: Beyond Pizza Hut
20	Expand Your Entertainment Options: Movies That Don't Fall Under the 'Action/Adventure' Category
21	Yours, Mine, Ours: Sharing the Remote Control.

22	'I Could Have Played a Better Game Than That!': Why Women Laugh
23	Adventures in Housekeeping I: Let's Clean the Cupboard
24	Adventures in Housekeeping II: Let's Clean Under the Bed
25	'I Don't Know': Be the First Man to Say It!
26	Directions: It's OK to Ask for Them
27	Listening: It's Not Just Something You Do During Halftime
28	Accepting Your Limitations: Just Because You Have Power Tools Doesn't Mean You Can Fix It

TRAMP

A tramp asks a man for $2.
The man says, 'If I give you $2, will you buy booze with it?'
The tramp says: 'No.'
The man asks, 'Will you gamble it away?'
The tramp says: 'No.'
The man asks: 'Will you come home with me then, so my wife can see what happens to a man who doesn't drink and doesn't gamble?'

TRASH

How do you know when a woman is really trashy? She brings a date to her own wedding.

TRUST

How can you trust a woman, when she bleeds for five days and still not die?

T-SHIRT SLOGANS

'I Used Up All My Sick Days ... So I Called In Dead.'

'Husband and Cat Lost... Reward for Cat.'

'Happiness Is Seeing Your Mother-in-Law on a Missing Person Ad.'

'Just Give Me Chocolate and Nobody Gets Hurt.'

'Learn from Your Parents' Mistakes ... Use Birth Control.'

'If God Had Wanted Me to Touch My Toes, He Would Have Put Them on My Knees.'

'Wrinkled Was Not One of the Things I Wanted to Be When I Grew Up.'

'If You Remember the '60s, You Weren't Really There.'

(Across a drawing of a skeleton) 'Waiting for the Perfect Man.'

'My Wife and I Married for Better or Worse ... She Couldn't Do Better and I Couldn't Do Worse.'

'The More I Learn About Women, the More I Love My Harley.'

'Filthy Stinking Rich ... Well, Two Out of Three Isn't Bad.'

TURDS

(Punching out a big one in the undies, Dropping an egg, Splattering the porcelain, Dropping a darkie, Clogging up the S Bend, Giving birth to a teacher)

'Mozza' was walking in the dark along a road to a mates place. He suddenly had an urgent need to shit. He moved to the side of the road. Dropped his overalls and crapped. With the job done he pulled his overalls back on and proceeded on his way, leaving the turd in the dark right beside the bitumen. When he arrived at his mates place a party was in full progress, so he wanders in, but was soon made aware by all others present that he stank to high hell. An investigation soon discovered that the turd 'Mozza' thought was beside the bitumen had in fact landed in his overalls, when he squatted. His mates still talk of it.

In a Victorian country town there appears an inclination on the men folk to drop turds wherever. 'Pouch' was heading home from the pub in the dark. Walking past the local garage, Mongrel Motors, he decided he needed to have a shit so dropped his dacks beside the bitumen. The next morning 'LeRoy' was walking his greyhound and spots the human turd sitting proudly beside the bitumen. He was disgusted and later reported to 'Pouch' that some dirty bastard had had a crap in the street beside 'Mongrel Motors'.

'Pouch' didn't have the heart to tell his mate it was him. To this day 'LeRoy' is none-the-wiser!

Bob Medwell was skinny dipping with his girlfriend, and a mate and his missus at a reservoir not far from a regional town in Victoria. Darkness came and so it was decided to head home. All got out of the water except Bob.

After a while of dead quietness, he yells out excitedly, 'Hey, I've caught a bloody brown trout, come and have a look at it.'

His mate walked back in the water and made his way through the darkness.

Bob wades up. 'Stick your hands out and I'll put it in but make sure you get a good grip of the bugger, it's still alive.'

Not suspecting anything the mate puts out his hands in anticipation. Bob slaps a fresh turd in his mate's hands! The bastard had dropped a turd in the water, and retrieved it as it floated away. Foul language and laughter ...

Why is a woman like a dog turd?
The older it is, the easier it is to pick up.

A party was in full swing. Everyone was pissed and hooning about. There was an old outside shithouse down the yard. Blokes were lying about on the lawn. If one bloke has a piss you can bet others will follow. Wedlow was first to get up.

His mates joined him in a piss, urine spraying everywhere. Wedlow decided he could piss over the roof of the dunny. He lets out a grunt and it was evident he was really going to give it his best. He tried so hard to push it out of his bladder that he laid a nugget in his undies.

TV

'What's on TV?' asked the wife.
'Dust' replied the husband.

TWATS

Women have two holes so when they get drunk you can carry them like a six pack.

How do you know when you're screwing your woman too much?
Stick your thumb in her arse hole, and middle finger up her snatch. If you can snap your fingers ease off with the screwing a bit

TYRE MAN

The head of a major tyre company was doing his rounds of his stores. He was picked up at Tullamarine Airport by the manager of one of the stores. Parked at the stoplights leaving the airport, when a hotted up Commodore with loud thumping music pulled up beside them.

In the car were a few young hoods with beanies pulled down over their ears. The lights change green and the hoons scream of in a cloud of smoke and screaming tyres. The manager says disgustingly, 'Bloody idiots.'

The Tyreman smiles and replies, 'No mate, they're playing my song. That's music to my ears.'

U

UGLY

A woman is really ugly when a cannibal looks at her and orders a salad.

How can a woman tell if she is ugly?
When men only want to play dress poker with her.

How do you know if a man has an ugly wife?
Her nickname is Spot.

UNDER OATH

'You seem to have more than the average share of intelligence for a man of your background,' sneered the lawyer at a witness on the stand. '

'If I wasn't under oath, I'd return the compliment,' replied the witness.

UNDIES

Bloke goes to the doctor for a complete checkup. Doctor examines him, then says, 'OK, I want a urine sample, a faeces sample and a sperm sample.'

The bloke says, 'Look Doc, I'm in a bit of a hurry, can I just leave you my undies?'

UNFORGETTABLE WEDDING

If any of you blokes out there have ever thought you have balls, forget about it. This is a true story that just happened at a wedding. This was a huge wedding with about 300 guests (for you rich folk, this is huge by middle-class standards).

At the reception, the groom got up on stage at the microphone to talk to the crowd. He said that he wanted to thank everyone for coming, many from long distances, to support them at their wedding. He especially wanted to thank the bride and groom's families for coming, and to thank everyone for coming and bringing gifts. He wanted in return to give everyone a gift from him. So taped to the bottom of everyone's chair was a manila envelope. That was his gift to everyone, and he told them to open it.

Inside the manila envelope was an 8 x 10 photograph of his best man having sex with the bride. (He must have grown suspicious of them and hired a private detective to trail them and take the photographs.)

After he had stood there and watched people's reactions for a couple of minutes, he turned to the best man and said, 'Fuck you', turned to the bride and said, 'Fuck you', and then said, 'I'm out of here.' He got the marriage annulled the next day.

URINALS

(dunny, piss trough, carzy)

The types you may meet in the men's dunny:
EXCITABLE: Jocks half twisted around, cannot find hole, rips jocks.
SOCIABLE: Joins friends in piss whether he has to or not.
CROSSEYED: Looks into next urinal to see how the other guy is fixed.
TIMID: Can't piss if someone's watching, flushes urinal, comes back later.
SHY: Goes into cubicle, locks door, has piss only, waits a while and leaves
INDIFFERENT (Casual): All urinals being used, pisses in sink.
CLEVER (Smart Arse): No hands, whistles, fixes tie, looks around and usually pisses on floor.
WORRIED: Not sure of where he has been lately, makes quick inspection.
FRIVOLOUS: Plays stream up, down and across urinals, tries to hit fly or bug.
ABSENT-MINDED: Opens vest, pulls out tie, pisses in pants.
CHILDISH: Pisses directly in bottom of urinal, likes to see it bubble.
SNEAK: Farts silently while pissing, acts very innocent, knows man in next stall will get blamed.
PATIENT: Stands very close for a long while waiting, reads with free hand.
DESPERATE: Waits in long line, teeth floating, pisses in pants.
TOUGH (Show Off): Bangs dick on side of urinal to dry it.
EFFICIENT: Waits until he has to crap, then does both.

FAT: Backs up and takes a blind shot at urinal, pisses in shoe.
LITTLE: Stands on box, falls in, drowns.
DRUNK: Holds right thumb in left hand, pisses in pants.
DISGRUNTLED: Stands for a while, grunts, farts, walks away.
CONCEITED: Holds two-inch dick like a baseball bat.
RADICAL: Ignores urinal. Pisses on wall.

URINATE

More men's lingo: to point Percy at the porcelain, splash the boots, syphon the python, give-the-one-eyed-trouser-snake-a-drink, dangle the doodle, throttle the ferret, give the dog a walk, maul the mutton.

A girl and her bloke were out for a drive in the country when she decided she needed to pee. He pulled over and she jumped out of the car. Ten minutes later she came back puffed and red faced saying, 'I can't go here; there is nowhere to hide.'

He drove a bit further until there was a tree in the distance, she leapt out, this time more frantic, only to return 15 minutes later saying the tree wasn't wide enough and someone might drive past and see her. He was bloody annoyed but he kept driving until they came to a bridge. He told her to sit over the edge and it would literally be just a drop in the ocean.

Thirty minutes later she hadn't come back. He was getting concerned, not to mention pissed off, so he went up to her and she signalled him to be quiet. 'Shhhh! There are people down there in a canoe and I can't go until they have passed.'

He looked over the edge, jumped up and yelled, 'That's not a canoe, stupid bitch, that's your reflection.'

V

VACUUM

How many men does it take to fix a vacuum cleaner?
None. Why the hell should we fix something we never use.

What is a man's idea of helping around the house?
Lifting his legs while you vacuum.

VIAGRA

An elderly gentleman went to the local drug store and asked the pharmacist for Viagra. The pharmacist said, 'That's no problem. How many do you want?'
   The man answered, 'Just a few, maybe four, but cut each one in four pieces.'
   The pharmacist said, 'That won't do you any good.'
   The elderly gentleman said, 'That's all right. I don't need them for sex any more as I am over 80 years old. I just want it to stick out far enough so I don't pee on my shoes.'

VIETNAMESE ROBBERY

How do you know if it was a Vietnamese who robbed your house?
Because your dog is missing and your homework's done.

VIRGINS

A young virgin couple are finally wed. Each one is nervous about the impending night, but neither is willing to admit it or to ask each other about it. Wondering what to do first, the young man calls his father.

'Pop, what do I do first?'
'Get naked and climb into bed,' his father replies. So, the young man does as he is advised.

The girl is mortified and calls her mama.
'Get naked and join him,' is the advice from mama, so she complies.

After lying there for a few moments, the young man excuses himself and calls his dad again.

'What do I do?' he asks.

His father replies, 'Look at her naked body. Then, take the hardest part of your body and put it where she pees!' is the dad's advice.

A few moments later, the girl again calls her mama.

'What do I do now?' she asks.

'Well, what is he doing?' mama asks.
'He's in the bathroom, dunking his head in the toilet.'

VOICES

A woman opened the door of a building and was about to step outside when she heard a voice saying, 'Don't take that next step or you'll regret it.' She paused and a brick came crashing to the pavement right where she would have been standing. She looked around and there was no one nearby.

The next day this woman was about to step into the street when she heard the same voice say, 'Don't take that next step or you'll regret it.' As she paused a truck came racing by and smashed into a nearby vehicle. She knew if she hadn't listened to that voice she would have been hurt badly, or maybe even killed. She looked behind her and there was no one nearby.

'All right,' she said, 'Who are you?'

'I'm your guardian angel,' the voice replied.

'Oh, if that's the case,' the woman said, 'Where were you on my wedding day?'

W

WANKER

A man was on a business trip staying in a fancy five-star hotel in Sydney. When he goes up to his room there's a sign near the bed that says 'Try our Massage Service'. So he rings down to the reception and books a massage. About ten minutes later a Japanese lady comes up and starts giving him a massage.

He's lying on his stomach and getting pretty horny and he gets a huge boner. She tells him to turn over and when he does she sees his cock standing to attention. So she giggles and says, 'Ahh, you want wanky!'

He says, 'Oooh, yes!' So she runs off into the bathroom and he lies on the bed waiting.

A few minutes later she sticks her head out from behind the bathroom door and asks, 'You finished yet?'

An Aussie tourist arrived in New Zealand, hired a car and set off for the wilderness. On his way he saw a bloke having sex with a sheep. Horrified, he pulled up at the nearest pub and ordered a straight Scotch.

Just as he was about to throw it back, he saw a bloke with one leg masturbating furiously at the bar. 'God!' the bloke cried, 'What the heck is going on here? I've been here one hour and I've seen a bloke banging a sheep, and now some bloke's spanking himself in the bar!'

'Fair go, mate,' the bartender told him, 'You can't expect a man with one leg to catch a sheep.'

WASTE

What do you call the space between a woman's tits and vagina?
Waist (waste).

Why do they call a woman's waist a waste?
Because you could easily fit another pair of tits in there.

WATERMELONS

A farmer in the country has a watermelon patch and upon inspection he discovers that some of the local kids have been helping themselves to a feast. The farmer thinks of ways to discourage this profit eating situation. So he puts up a sign that reads:

'WARNING; ONE OF THESE WATERMELONS CONTAINS CYANIDE!'

The farmer returns a week later to discover that none of the watermelons has been eaten, but now there is another sign next to his. It reads, 'NOW THERE ARE TWO!'

WEATHERMAN

A husband and his wife were sound asleep in bed when suddenly the phone rang. The husband picked up the phone and said, 'Hello? How the fuck do I know? What do I sound like, a weatherman?'

He slammed the phone down and settled back into bed.

'Who was that?' asked his wife.

'I don't know. Just some bloke who wanted to know if the coast was clear.'

WEDDINGS

Put me in charge of organising the wedding and ...

There would be a 'Rehearsal Dinner Keg' Party

Bridesmaids would wear matching blue jean cut-offs and halter tops. They would have NO tan lines and more skin showing than not.

Tuxes would have team logos on the back and the Nike shoes would have matching team colours.

All weddings would be banned that coincided with any football grand final.

Vows would mention cooking and sex specifically but omit that 'forsaking all others' part.

The couple would leave the ceremony in a 'hot' '73 Charger with racing tyres and flame designs on the side of the car. Better yet, on a Harley!

Idiots that tried to dance with the bride (unless they were really old) would get punched in the head.

Big slobbery dogs would be eligible for the role of 'Best Man'.

There would be 'Tailgate Receptions'.

Ceremonies would be short and honeymoons would be long.

Ceremonies and honeymoons would be inexpensive compared with the cost of the bachelor party. Those strippers and liquor sure do add up.

Men wouldn't ask, 'Well, what do you think, dear, the burgundy or the wine-coloured napkins?' They'd just grab extras from their local pub or tavern.

Favours would be matchbooks and cigars. Better yet, free drink passes at the local lounge.

The bride's dress would show cleavage, her navel and be formfitted to her arse.

Instead of a sit-down dinner or buffet, there would be a hog roast or buckets of chicken, pizza and plenty of barbecue.

No one would bother with that 'veil routine'. But they would insist the garter be as high up on her leg as it would go.

The bridal bouquet could be recycled from a previous funeral or something.

Invitations would read as follows: Tom (Dick or Harry) is getting the old ball and chain ... He's getting married.
He (circle which applicable)
a) knocked her up
b) couldn't get a different roommate, or
c) caved in to her ultimatum.
Please meet the woman who will cook and clean for him for the rest of his life at
a) Southern Stand, MCG
b) Bluey's Weekly Beer and Prawn night
c) Half-time during Sunday's Game
Please join us at the MoonLight Lounge after the game
For Beer, Nachos and Pizza. Oh Yeah, and BYOG.

WEIGHT

How do you screw a fat chick?
You jerk off in your hand and then throw it at her.

How can you tell if a woman is really fat?
Her front door has stretch marks.

How can you tell if a woman is really fat?
She goes to Japan and sumo wrestlers cower in fear.

Why do Japanese sumo wrestlers shave their legs?
So you can tell them apart from the feminists.

How does a woman knows she is overweight?
She's lying on the beach and people from
Greenpeace try to push her back into the sea.

Why is a fat woman like a moped?
Because they are fun to ride but you wouldn't want
your mates to see you riding either.

You can tell a woman is fat when her young lovers
try to carve their initials into her legs.

WHACKERS

Lingo: crazy, zany, stupid, goofy, idiotic, screwball, witless, loony, maudlin, bats, nuts, cuckoo, mad, daft, silly, dumb, irrational, peculiar, eccentric or amusing person.

A few bob short of a quid, kangaroo missing in the top paddock, minus some buttons, the motor's running but the battery's stuffed, bats in the belfry, hasn't got both oars in the water, a penny short of a pound, ten cents short of a buck, the lights are on but no one is home.

And see How to be a whacker, page 172.

WHAT EVERY MAN EXPECTS IN A WIFE

She will always be beautiful and cheerful.
She could marry a movie star, but wants only you.
She will have hair that never needs curlers or beauty shops.
Her beauty won't run in a rainstorm.
She will never be sick — just allergic to jewelry and fur coats.
She will insist that moving the furniture by herself, it's good for her figure.
She will be an expert in cooking, cleaning house, fixing the car or TV, painting the house, and keeping quiet.

Her favourite hobbies will be mowing the lawn.
She will hate credit cards.
Her favourite expression will be, 'What can I do for you, dear?'
She will think you have Einstein's brain but look like Mr Australia.
She will wish you would go out with the boys so that she could get some sewing done.
She will love you because you're so sexy.

WHAT HE USUALLY GETS

She speaks 140 words a minute, with gusts up to 180.
She was once a model for a totem pole.
Where there's smoke, there she is — cooking.
She's a light eater — once it gets light, she starts eating.
She lets you know you only have two faults: everything you do, and everything you say.
No matter what she does with it, her hair looks like an explosion in a steel wool factory.
If you get lost, open your wallet and she'll find you.

WHAT MEN REALLY MEAN

I'm just not quite sure about that.
(Fucked if I know.)

I don't think anyone really cares.
(Who gives a rat's arse anyway.)

You're a bit of a flirt love.
(I think you're a slut and a cocksucker.)

He's certainly a bit different.
(He's a frigging poofter if ever I saw one.)

Please don't do that.
(Do that again ya' mongrel, and I'll break your bloody arm.)

There's something on your face.
(You're dribbling, you dumb cunt.)

WHAT PISSES ME OFF

People who point at their wrist while asking for the time.
I know where my watch is mate, where the hell is yours? Do I point at my crotch when I ask where the dunny is?

People who are willing to get off their arse to search the entire room for the TV remote because they refuse to walk to the TV and change the channel manually.

When people say, 'Oh you just want to have your cake and eat it too.'
What good is a frigging cake you can't eat?

When people say, 'It's always in the last place you look.'
Why the fuck would you keep looking after you've found it?

When people say, while watching a movie, 'Did you see that?'
No fuckwit, I paid $12.00 to come to the theatre and stare at the fucking ceiling up there.

People who ask, 'Can I ask you a question?'
Didn't really give me a choice there, did you, mate?

When something is 'new and improved', which is it? If it's new, then there has never been anything before it. If it's an improvement, then there must have been something wrong with it before.

When a cop pulls you over and then asks if you know how fast you were going.
You should know, arsehole, you're the one who pulled me over.

WHAT?

What's the definition of mixed emotions?
When you see your mother-in-law backing off a cliff in your new car.

What do you do to double the value of a Datsun?
You fill it with petrol.

What's the difference between a blonde and a mosquito?
A mosquito stops sucking when you smack it.

What do you see when you look into a blonde's eyes?
The back of her head.

What is an organ grinder?
Sand in a condom.

What did the blonde say when she found out she was pregnant?
'I wonder if it's mine?'

What do you call twenty blondes in a circle?
A dope ring.

What do you do with a bachelor who thinks he's God's gift?
Exchange him.

What's a man's idea of foreplay?
Half an hour of begging.

What makes men chase women they have no intention of marrying?
The same urge that make dogs chase cars they have no intention of driving.

What should you give a man who has everything?
A woman to show him how to work it.

What does woman of 35 think of? Having children.
What does a man of 35 think of? Dating children.

What has four legs and an arm?
A happy pit-bull.

What is the thinnest book in the world?
What Men Know About Women.

WHAT'S THE DIFF?

What's the difference between a paycheck and a dick?
You don't have to beg a woman to blow your paycheck.

What's the difference between a new husband and a new dog?
After a year, the dog is still excited to see you.

What's the difference between a lawyer and God?
God doesn't think he's a lawyer.

WHINGE

'This treatment by an old friend and colleague has puzzled and wounded me. I am at loss to understand what I have done to deserve it.'
— Robert G. Menzies to prime minister John Gorton (not amused and embarrassed after being left stranded overseas as a result of a decision taken by the Gorton government to cut his travel perks

WHY

Why do women close their eyes during sex?
They can't stand seeing a man have a good time.

Why do men die before their wives?
They want to.

Why did God create lesbians?
So feminists couldn't breed.

Why can't you trust woman?
How can you trust something that bleeds for five days and doesn't die.

Why do women rub their eyes when they get up in the morning?
They don't have balls to scratch.

Why haven't women been to the moon?
It doesn't need cleaning.

Why is a laundromat a bad place to pick up a woman?
If she can't afford her own washing machine, she can't afford to keep you.

Why are there so many Smiths in the phone book?
They all have phones.

Why do blondes have more fun?
They are easier to amuse.

Why don't blind people skydive?
Because it scares the hell out of the dog.

Why can't Miss Piggy count to 70?
Because every time she gets to 69 she gets a frog in her throat.

Why do you need a driver's licence to buy liquor when you can't drink and drive?

Why are there flotation devices under plane seats instead of parachutes?

Why are cigarettes sold in gas stations when smoking is prohibited there?

If a convenience store is open 24 hours a day, 365 days a year, why are there locks on the doors?

Why is it that when you transport something by car, it's called a shipment, but when you transport something by ship, it's called cargo?

You know that little indestructible black box that is used on planes? Why can't they make the whole plane out of the same substance?

Why is it that when you're driving and looking for an address, you turn down the volume on the radio?

Why are husbands like lawn mowers?
They're hard to get started, emit foul odours and don't work half the time.

Why do men like love at first sight?
It saves them a lot of time.

Why do some spiders kill their males after mating?
To stop the snoring before it starts.

Why don't men have mid-life crises?
They're stuck in adolescence.

Why is sleeping with a man like a soap opera?
Just when it's getting interesting, they're finished until next time.

Why do men find it difficult to make eye contact?
Breasts don't have eyes.

Why do bachelors like smart women?
Opposites attract.

When I was in primary school, all I wanted was a girl with big tits. In high school, I dated a girl with big tits, but there was no passion.

So I decided I needed a passionate girl.

At university, I dated a passionate girl, but she was too emotional. I decided I needed a girl with some stability.

I found a very stable girl, but she was boring. She never got excited about anything. So I decided I needed a girl with some excitement.

I found an exciting girl, but I couldn't keep up with her. She rushed from one thing to another, never settling on anything. She was directionless. So I decided to find a girl with some ambition.

After university, I found an ambitious girl and married her. She was so ambitious, she divorced me and took everything I owned.

Now all I want is a girl with big tits.

WHY DOUGH IS BETTER THAN A COCK

It's enjoyable soft or hard.
It makes a mess too, but it tastes better.
It doesn't mind if you take your anger out on it.
You always want to swallow.
It won't complain if you share it with your friends.
It's quick and convenient.
You can enjoy it more than once.
It comes already protectively wrapped.
You can make it as large as you want.
If you don't finish it you can save it for later.
It's easier to get the kind you want.
You can comparison shop.
It's easier to find in a grocery store.
You can put it away when you've had enough.
You know yours has never been eaten before.
It won't complain if you chew on it.
It comes chocolate flavoured.
You always know when to get rid of it.

You can return it — satisfaction guaranteed.
It's always ready to go.
You won't get arrested if you eat it in public.
You don't have to change the sheets if you eat it in bed.
It won't wake you up because it's hard.
You don't have to find an excuse not to eat it.
You can tell your friends how much you've eaten without sounding like you're bragging.
It won't take up room in your bed.
You never have unwanted dough chasing you around.
You know what the extra weight is from.
It won't get jealous if you pick up another one.
It never has an insecurity problem with its size.

WIFE

Losing a wife can be hard. In my case damned near impossible.

I haven't spoken to my wife for 18 months. I don't like to interrupt her.

What's a wife?
An attachment you screw on the bed to get the housework done.

If your wife keeps coming out ot he kitchen to nag you, what have you done wrong?
Made her chain too long.

WINE

A woman was brought before the courts. Her husband is in the witness box being cross-examined.

'So, Mr Smith, tell the court why you brought your wife before the court?'

'Well, I just said, "Man is like a good wine, matures with age", and with that she locked me in the cellar!'

WISE GUY

One day an old man gets on a bus. Several minutes later a punk kid with red and orange hair gets on. The kid notices the old man staring at him.

The kid looks at him and says, 'What are you staring at, old man. Haven't you done anything wild in your time?'

The old guy replies, 'Yes, I fucked a parrot once. I was just wondering if you were my kid!'

WISE MEN

Why wasn't Jesus born in Perth?
Because God couldn't find three wise men from the east!

WOMAN'S VIEW

What did God say after creating man?
'I must be able to do better than that.'

What did God say after creating Eve?
'Practice makes perfect.'

How many honest, intelligent, caring men in the world does it take to do the dishes?
Both of them.

Why don't women blink during foreplay?
They don't have time.

Why does it take a million sperm to fertilise one egg?
They won't stop to ask directions.

What do men and sperm have in common?
They both have a one-in-a-million chance of becoming a human being.

How does a man show that he is planning for the future?
He buys two cases of beer.

What is the difference between men and government bonds?
The bonds mature.

How many men does it take to change a roll of toilet paper?
We don't know; it has never happened.

Why is it difficult to find men who are sensitive, caring and good-looking?
They all already have boyfriends.

What do you call a woman who knows where her husband is every night?
A widow.

When do you care for a man's company?
When he owns it.

Why are married women heavier than single women?
Single women come home, see what's in the fridge and go to bed.
Married women come home, see what's in bed and go to the fridge

How do you get a man to do sit-ups?
Put the remote control between his toes.

What is the one thing that all men at singles bars have in common?
They're married.

WOMEN ARE:

Why are women like screen doors?
After they've been banged a few times, they loosen up.

Why are women like parking spaces?
The best ones are taken, the rest are handicapped.

Why are women like rocks?
The flat ones are better to skip.

Man says to God: 'God, why did you make woman so beautiful?'
God says: 'So you would love her.'
Man says: 'But God, why did you make her so dumb?'
God says: 'So she would love you.'

WOMEN OF THE WORLD

From 13 to 18 a woman is like Africa — virgin and unexplored.
From 19 to 35 she is like Asia — hot and exotic.
From 36 to 45 she is like America — fully explored and free with her resources.
From 46 to 55 she is like Europe — exhausted, but still has points of interest.
From 56 on she is like Australia — everyone knows it's down there but no one gives a damn.

WONG SIZE

A senior nurse at a Brisbane hospital was instructing a new nurse in her duties. 'Now go down to bed 12 and give the gentleman there, Mr Wong, a bed bath. Make sure you do him all over. And dear, don't worry when you see his penis, because he has tattooed his name on it. Just ignore it and don't laugh.'

Some time later, the young nurse returns looking rather embarrassed.

'So how did you go with Mr Wong, nurse?'
'His name isn't Wong — it's Wollongong!'

WORK

For years I've been blaming it on iron, poor blood, lack of vitamins, dieting and a dozen other maladies. But now I have found out the real reason. I'm tired because I'm overworked. The population of this country is 18 million. 8 million are retired. That leaves 10 million to do the work. There are 6 million in school, which leaves 4 million to do the work. Of this there are 2 million employed by the federal government. This leaves 2 million to do the work. Half-a-million are in the forces, which leaves 1.5 million to do the work. Take from this the total of 1 million people who work for state and local government, and that leaves 500,000 to do the work. There are 260,000 in hospitals, so that leaves 240,000 to do the work. And, there are 228,000 people on welfare, that leaves 12,000 to do the work. Now, there are 11,998 people in prisons. That leaves just two people to do the work. You and me. And you're sitting there messing around reading a book!

WORMS

A young boy spots a worm sticking its nose out of the ground and he pulls it out. His grandfather says: 'You shouldn't have done that. The worm will be eaten by a bird.' The boy is upset so the grandfather tells him that he'll give him a dollar if he can think of a way to get the worm back into the ground. The boy runs off to the house but soon returns carrying a can of spray-starch. He holds up the worm and sprays it with the starch, which makes it go stiff. He then pushes the worm back into its hole and collects his dollar.

The next morning the boy is playing out in the yard. His grandfather comes up to him and hands him ten dollars and says: 'That's from your grandmother.'

How do you tell which end of a worm is the head? Bury it in flour and wait till it farts.

X

WINNER 1999 QUEENSLAND SPELLING CONTEST

They called it Four X because Queenslanders can't spell BEER!
—'Ted' (an ex-southerner, main bar, The Royal, Dalby, Qld)

Y

YOU KNOW

You have kleptomania, when you take something for it.

You know some days you're the pigeon, and some days you're the statue.

You can please only one person per day. Today is not your day. Tomorrow isn't looking good either.

On the keyboard of life, always keep one finger on the escape key.

Stupidity got you into this mess — why can't it get you out?

You don't mind going nowhere as long as it's an interesting path.

You know indecision is the key to flexibility.

You know in just two days, tomorrow will be yesterday.

You considered atheism but there weren't enough holidays.

You always wanted to be a procrastinator, never got around to it.

Your inferiority complex is not as good as mine.

Z

ZIPS

In a crowded city, at a crowded bus stop, a young woman was waiting for the bus. She was decked out in a tight leather mini-skirt with matching tight leather boots and jacket. As the bus rolled up and it became her turn to get on the bus, she became aware that her skirt was too tight to climb up on the bus's first step. So, slightly embarrassed and with a quick smile to the bus driver, she reached behind her, unzipped her skirt a little, thinking that this would give her enough slack to raise her leg.

Again, she tried to step onto the bus, only to discover she still could not make the step. So, a little more embarrassed, she reached behind and unzipped her skirt a little more.

And for the third time she attempted the step, and once again, much to her chagrin, she could not get her leg high enough because of the tight skirt.

With a coy smile to the driver, she unzipped the offending skirt to give even more slack, but still she was unable to make the step.

About this time the man behind her in the queue, picked her up easily from the waist and placed her lightly on the step of the bus.

Well, she went ballistic and turned on the would-be hero, screeching at him, 'How dare you touch my body! I don't even know who you are!'

'Well ma'am, normally I would agree with you, but after you unzipped my fly three times, I figured that we were friends!'

Squark!

Strewth, those jokes will be about as popular as a fart in a phone box!